INDIGENOUS PEOPLES DAY

Handbook for Activists
& Documentary History

Indigenous Peoples Day Committee

Special thanks to all who
made generous contributions to this publication.

INDIGENOUS PEOPLES DAY

Handbook for Activists
& Documentary History

Celebrate this annual holiday with us
in honor of all of our ancestors,
the people continuing the struggle today,
and future generations

Indigenous Peoples Day Committee

Curated by John Curl

Berkeley
<u>Indigenous Peoples Day Coordinators</u>
1992 Dennis Jennings
1993 Lee Sprague
1994 John Bellinger
1995-1999 Millie Ketcheshawno
2000-2004 Sharilane Suke
2005-2006 Rochelle Hayes
2007-2017 Gino Barichello

ISBN-13: 978-1539952213
ISBN-10: 1539952215

Indigenous Peoples Day Press, Berkeley, CA.
http://ipdpow wow.org

Cover photography and design:
Megan Padilla - Megan Elizabeth Media

Printed in the United States of America.

CONTENTS

Dedicated to the spirit of Millie Ketcheshawno,
a founder of Indigenous Peoples Day

INTRODUCTION

At sunrise on Friday, October 12, 1492, a group of Taino people gathered on the tropical sands of Guanahani, a small Caribbean island, to watch three very foreign ships lower a small boat which carried their captains to shore.

From the log by Christopher Columbus:

> "As I saw that they were very friendly to us..., I presented them with some red caps, and strings of beads to wear upon the neck, and many other trifles of small value, wherewith they were much delighted, and became wonderfully attached to us. Afterwards they came swimming to the boats, bringing parrots, balls of cotton thread, javelins, and many other things which they exchanged for articles we gave them, such as glass beads, and hawk's bells... Weapons they have none, nor are acquainted with them, for I showed them swords which they grasped by the blades, and cut themselves through ignorance... They are all of a good size and stature, and handsomely formed... It appears to me, that the people are ingenious, and would be good servants... I intend at my return to carry home six of them to your Highnesses..."[1]

That was the first encounter of two worlds, as seen through the eyes of one of the protagonists.

Columbus's narrative continues the next morning:

"Saturday, 13 October.
At daybreak great multitudes... came to the ship in canoes, made of a single trunk of a tree, wrought in a wonderful

manner...; some of them large enough to contain forty or forty-five men, others of different sizes down to those fitted to hold but a single person... I was very attentive to them, and strove to learn if they had any gold. Seeing some of them with little bits of this metal hanging at their noses, I gathered from them by signs that by going southward or steering round the island in that direction, there would be found a king who possessed large vessels of gold, and in great quantities."

Thus cataclysmic events were set in motion that forever changed the land that Native people call Turtle Island, and maps call the Americas. One year later, Columbus returned with the Spanish army and began the conquest.

Fast forward exactly five hundred more years, and in 1992, Berkeley, California became the first city in the world to officially commemorate and celebrate that October 12th encounter as Indigenous Peoples Day.

•

The Quincentenary

The spark that touched off Indigenous Peoples Day in Berkeley was the Bay Area being designated by the US Congress as the center of a planned gala national celebration of the 500th anniversary of October 12, 1492.

To organize the Bay Area activities, an independent non-profit committee was set up under the joint honorary chair of the mayors of San Francisco, Oakland, and San Jose, and told by the U.S. Columbus Commission that it needed to raise and contribute $1.5 million.

The U.S. Columbus Quincentenary Jubilee Commission had been established by the US Congress, and signed into law by President Reagan in 1984, "to plan, encourage, coordinate and conduct the commemoration of the voyages of Christopher Columbus." They cut a deal for Spain to build replicas of the three ships, and sail them across the ocean to Miami. The Commission would then take over, and oversee an extensive 20-city US tour along the east coast, gulf coast, and west coast, with most expenses

8

absorbed by the tour cities. The US government gave the commission $1 million, and the rest of their budget was to be filled by corporations, with Texaco pledging $5 million.

TUESDAY, AUGUST 11, 1992

Santa Maria, Pinta and Nina replicas.

Oakland Tribune 10/11/1992
The replicas of Columbus's ships in Boston harbor, August, 1992.

The Niña, Pinta, and Santa Maria replicas were scheduled to arrive in Miami in February, 1992, then sail around the southern tip of Florida, across the Gulf of Mexico to Corpus Christi, make a U-turn and wend their way back along the gulf coast, then up the east coast, arriving in Boston in August. The ships would then be hoisted onto barges, and towed down to Panama, through the canal, and up the west coast. Right outside San Francisco Bay, the ships were to be launched again, due west across the bay from Berkeley. The three ships were to sail triumphantly under the majestic Golden Gate bridge into the bay on October 12, 1992 as the national focal point and centerpiece of the grand hoopla.

Like the Tainos on Guanahani in 1492, we in the Bay Area saw Columbus coming at us and we had to deal with him.

(For more on the Quincentenary, and how didn't happen as they planned, see page 71.)

•

9

About This Book

This is both a documentary history and an oral history, a compilation of how we did it, and a practical manual or guidebook of sorts, with some cautionary tales. This book aims at being useful to people everywhere who want to celebrate Indigenous Peoples Day in your own corner of the world. It is coming out as we approach the 25th anniversary of the first Berkeley Indigenous Peoples Day, 1992-2017, which is also the 525th anniversary of the European intrusion into the Americas, 1492-2017.

•

Indigenous Peoples Day Around The Country

Other U.S. cities and states have since joined in celebrating Indigenous Peoples Day, including Seattle, Minneapolis, Denver, Phoenix, Santa Cruz, Sebastopol, Nevada City, Madison, Richmond (CA), Vermont, and Alaska. Indigenous Peoples Day is also celebrated in numerous communities by groups, organizations, schools, tribes, and friends. Indigenous Peoples Day is a fast growing movement.

In addition, South Dakota celebrates Native American Day and Hawaii now honors the Polynesian explorers.

•

Three Landmarks

Participants in social movements need to know their movement's history and roots. Numerous hands and minds created Indigenous Peoples Day and some have already walked on, taking with them irreplaceable memory and knowledge. This book is also an attempt to collect some memories and knowledge, and pass them on, to document some of the landmarks along the way for Indigenous Peoples Day, and to give credit to some of the many contributors.

Three important Indigenous conferences played a central role in creating Indigenous Peoples Day:

1. It was first proposed by Native representatives at a United Nations Indigenous conference in Geneva in 1977.

2. It was re-ignited in 1990 at the first Continental Gathering of Indigenous Peoples in Quito, Ecuador.

3. Finally, Indigenous Peoples Day was given immediacy in 1991 by the All-Native Conference at D-Q University, which morphed into the All Peoples Network Conference at Oakland's Laney College, where the Resistance 500 coalition was created.

So many people have made important contributions to Indigenous Peoples Day over the many years, that it is not possible to thank all by name here. Your spirits are still very much with us. Several important members of our committee who have walked on and are still guiding us include Millie Ketcheshawno, Don Littlecloud Davenport, and Mark Gorrell.

•

Roots of NonNative People

What about those of us who did not come from Indigenous blood or culture? Modern American mass society is still based on a colonial mind set, and has not yet made its peace with this continent: we are on it but not yet of it. We have not yet learned how to live in indigenous American ways. To learn the right ways of living on Turtle Island, nonIndigenous Americans can begin by making our peace with history and with the Native peoples. Lost in the Euro-American version of liberty, has been community and sustainability. While we have gained in mobility, we have paid the heavy price of profound alienation, rootlessness, institutionalized social injustice, environmental devastation. The Native peoples' struggle for control of their communities and respect for Mother Earth can light the way.

Every society tells creation myths to its children, and the Euro-American creation myth that most of us learned as small children, is the Columbus story. I bought a children's book recently that lays it out just as I heard it many years ago. Columbus the visionary explorer stumbles on a New World where he is welcomed by people who are awed by Europe's superior cultural gifts. The children's story ends with Columbus returning to Spain with the amazing news.

But of course the reality was far different, and did not end there. Columbus returned to the New World with a great armada, and proceeded to conquer and plunder wherever he went. His own writings clearly show that this had always been his plan. Unable to find enough gold to fulfill the financial promises he'd made to his backers, Columbus rounded up Native Americans and sent them to be sold in the slave market in Seville. Christopher Columbus started slavery in the Americas and invented the trans-Atlantic slave trade.

Yet Native peoples have survived. Over five million people in the US today are all or part American Indian, and many of the 55 million Latinos in the US today are partly or wholly of indigenous descent.

In facing the realities of the European invasion of the Americas with all its pain, in accepting an historical narrative based on truth instead of lies, in looking for new constructive origin tales to pass on to our children, where is there to turn but backwards, to the very oldest stories of our hemisphere.

Here in the Americas (or on Turtle Island, or Abya Yala, as they say in the Andes), perhaps our greatest hope for a livable future lies in the ancient Incan vision that you can read on pages 92-94 of this book, the joining of the Condor's and Eagle's tears.

Roots of Indigenous Peoples Day

Indigenous Peoples Day springs from today's resurgence of Native peoples; from the exposure of the true history behind the Columbus mythology; from the deep yearnings of all caring people to move beyond the destructive culture of domination, exploitation, and greed, and to leave for our seventh generation grandchildren a peaceful, just, balanced, sustainable living world.

On Indigenous Peoples Day we celebrate the Native peoples and cultures of the world and their spirit of respect for the earth through living in sustainable ways, a philosophy that has kept Native cultures flourishing despite the hardships of the last centuries. Native American cultures are very varied, yet share that common philosophical core.

In past centuries Europeans chose to colonize other lands and exploit other peoples, instead of staying home and living with their neighbors in peace. The colonial project in the Americas over the last 525 years has cost countless lives. Christopher Columbus embodies that tragic history.

Indigenous Peoples Day is a time when Native and non-Native people can meet and mingle, get to know each other better, and gain deeper connections in the community. In many urban areas today, Native people are neighbors, although some nonNatives may not be very aware of it. In the Berkeley pow wow, everyone is invited to dance in the round dances, young and old of every ethnicity sharing the dance circle, and everyone can browse and converse their way through the Indian Market. This year we will be offering docent tours of the pow wow, led by Native people, to bridge nonNatives' understanding and participation.

People everywhere instinctively understand that the world needs to embrace Indigenous philosophy if future generations are to survive and flourish, and that is one of the reasons why so many communities are embracing Indigenous Peoples Day.

•

We invite you all to Berkeley Indigenous Peoples Day every year on the second Saturday in October, 10 am to 6 pm in Martin Luther King, Jr. Civic Center Park. Admission free. Join us in celebrating Indigenous culture and resurgence, and learning to live in indigenous ways.

•

Indigenous Peoples Day Committee
2017

Gino Barichello, Pow Wow Coordinator
Joaquin Cruz
John Curl
Nanette Deetz
Hallie Frazer, Vendors Coordinator
Nancy Gorrell
Venetia Moore
Megan Padilla
Sabah Williams

•

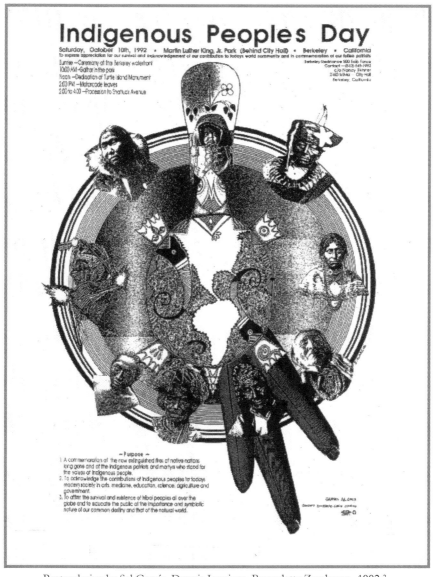

Poster design by Sal García, Dennis Jennings, Bernadette Zambrano. 1992 [2]

— Purpose —

1. A commemoration of the now extinguished fires of native nations long gone and of the indigenous patriots and martyrs who stood for the values of Indigenous people.

2. To acknowledge the contributions of indigenous peoples to today's modern society in arts, medicine, education, science, agriculture and government.

3. To affirm the survival and existence of tribal peoples all over the globe and to educate the public of the importance and symbiotic nature of our common destiny and that of the natural world.

Dennis Jennings, the city's Indigenous Peoples' Day coordinator, Mayor Loni Hancock and friends got together to observe Berkeley's new holiday.

[*Berkeley Voice* 10/15/1992]

STEPS TO BRINGING
INDIGENOUS PEOPLES DAY
INTO YOUR COMMUNITY

Collected by Nancy Gorrell

1. Gather like-minded people, meet and organize. Indigenous Peoples Day celebrates Native cultures, promotes sustainable ways of living in peace and harmony with the natural environment. Keep your focus positive.

2. Educate yourselves about Indigenous history and culture in your region, and the historical interactions between Native and nonNative people.

3. If the starting group is entirely nonNative, connect with Native people in your area, who bring life experiences and understandings that enrich any group. There may be more Native people in your community than you are aware of, and Native organizations can be brought in. Establish personal contact, invite them to join or be advisors.

4. The group should always strive for consensus, which means greater unity than simple majority decision-making. On questions of Indigenous culture, history, and other related issues, the nonNative people in your group should listen to the Native voices in your group, respect their judgment and learn from their perspective.

5. Study and understand the political process needed to have your community establish Indigenous Peoples Day as an official holiday. That could include the necessity of walking the concept through various commissions and boards before it reaches the ultimate decision-makers.

6. Meet with elected officials and commissioners, explain what you are doing and elicit their support. Make sure to include the school board and library.

7. Connect with organizations and people in your community you expect may be sympathetic. Speak at local meetings of every sort, and hand out informational flyers. Ask the support of the local business community, nonprofits, labor organizations. A nearby college can be the source of great resources and support.

8. Explain that people around the world today understand that the future of the planet depends on our all learning to live in Indigenous ways, and NonNative people can understand how to do that from the people who have been trying to live that way since time immemorial. Explain that Indigenous Peoples Day is a celebration of the timeless Native philosophy of living in peaceful sustainable communities based on sharing and cooperation, in balance with the natural environment. Remind them that October 12th is a commemoration of the encounter of Native people and Europeans that took place on October 12, 1492, on a small island in the Caribbean. Explain that Indigenous Peoples Day focuses the commemoration of that day on the extraordinary Indigenous civilization, and away from glamorizing the brutal colonial project that so badly damaged the land and Native peoples.

9. You don't need to wait for official recognition to begin to celebrate Indigenous Peoples Day. You can organize a celebration this year, which will serve to educate the community, and pave the way for official recognition.

10. Organize public events in the weeks and months leading up to Indigenous Peoples Day, as well as on the day itself. Publicize these in all the media. Organize events in the schools and libraries. Identify supportive individuals to help with access.

11. You can celebrate Indigenous Peoples Day in an infinite variety of ways. Design attractive posters and fliers. Make the most of social media. Go on radio and TV. Hang a banner across your main downtown street. Hold free events in easily-accessible venues, or right on the street, where people are. Include speakers, music, poetry, dance, art. So that children and working families can attend, your family-oriented events need to be on the weekend closest to October 12.

12. Make your first Indigenous Peoples Day an exciting, fun, and positive event. A family event. Bring out the truths of history, but focus on including all people in a brighter future. Recognize historical injustices, but let positivity shine through and elevate you. Your community will embrace your positive initiatives. A positive focus is the only way to make Indigenous Peoples Day a sustainable living holiday in your community.

13. Organize what works in your community, with the resources and population that exist. We in Berkeley and the East Bay have held a pow wow on Indigenous Peoples Day for over two decades, but a pow wow may not be an option in your area. Only the support and participation of the Bay Area Native community has made our pow wows possible.

14. As you read the history in this book, envision some of what worked for us, and transform it in creative ways to the unique situation in the community where you live today.

All our relations.

Collection of Gino Barichello

Members of the Indigenous Peoples Committee, around 2009 at an honor dance. L-R: Nancy Gorrell, Mark Gorrell, Don Littlecloud Davenport, Gino Barichello, Venetia Moore, John Curl, Bernardo Lopez.

CHAPTER ONE

The first Berkeley Indigenous Peoples Day, 1992

Through the course of 1991, the Berkeley Resistance 500 Task Force (our committee's proper name at that time) walked the concept of Indigenous Peoples Day through a number the city commissions until we finally reached the Berkeley City Council on October 22, 1991. On that date the city council voted unanimously to make Indigenous Peoples Day an official Berkeley holiday. In all the following years, the City has continued to sponsor and support Indigenous Peoples Day.

Many people think that Berkeley has always celebrated Indigenous Peoples Day with a pow wow, but that is not entirely true. We held our first pow wow in our second year. Our inaugural Berkeley Indigenous Peoples Day, our celebration in 1992, was different. Our 1992 activities involved many different cultural and educational events. Throughout that entire first year 1991-1992, we organized events at many different venues around the city and around the San Francisco Bay Area.

At that time, our organizing committee belonged to a coalition called Resistance 500, and we were also affiliated with the 1992 Bay Area Regional Indian Alliance (BARIA). Many groups, Indian and nonIndian, were actively working together in various cities around the Bay Area with the same mission of turning the Quincentennial 1492-1992 into a day of Indigenous celebration. Our organizing committee had a balance of Native and non-Native members. The Native people in our group were simultaneously active in BARIA, including our Berkeley coordinator, Dennis Jennings.

Since Indigenous Peoples Day is a community and family event, we decided to always celebrate it on the nearest Saturday, which in 1992 was October 10.

Here is how one of our flyers described our Indigenous Peoples Day program in that first year:

•

Berkeley's Quincentennial Commemoration of the 500 years 1492-1992 will be held on the first Indigenous Peoples Day, Saturday, October 10, 1992, with Representatives from many of the Native Nations of Turtle Island (Continental America)

Sunrise ceremony at the waterfront.

12 noon to 4 pm: commemoration activities in Martin Luther King, Jr. Park (Allston Way and M.L.K. Way), with cultural presentations by Indigenous people and participation by the Berkeley schools.

The Turtle Island Monument and time capsule storing Native thoughts and artifacts will be dedicated. Booths selling Indigenous food and crafts; informational tables from Native, Environmental, and Human Rights groups.

At 2 pm: procession leaves the park and slowly circles to Shattuck Avenue, with art installations and cultural presentations at each street corner on themes relating to the 500 years of Indigenous struggle and Resistance to colonialism. The procession will circle back to the park for closing ceremonies.

Berkeley's Quincentennial Commemoration of
the 500 years 1492-1992
will be held on the first

INDIGENOUS PEOPLES DAY

Saturday, October 10, 1992

with Representitives from many of

the Native Nations of Turtle Island

(Continental America)

Sunrise ceremony at the waterfront.

12 noon to 4 pm: commemoration activities in
Martin Luther King, Jr. Park (Allston Way and M.L.K. Way),
with cultural presentations by Indigenous people and
participation by the Berkeley schools.

The Turtle Island Monument and time capsule
storing Native thoughts and artifacts will be dedicated.

Booths selling Indigenous food and crafts; informational tables
from Native, Environmental, and Human Rights groups.

At 2 pm: procession leaves the park and slowly circles
to Shattuck Avenue, with art installations and cultural presentations
at each street corner on themes relating to the 500 years
of Indigenous struggle and resistance to colonialism.

The procession will circle back to the park for closing ceremonies.

This event can begin a profound annual tradition in Berkeley,
refocusing social consciousness
toward the nurturing leadership of Indigenous tradition
in harmony with the natural environment.

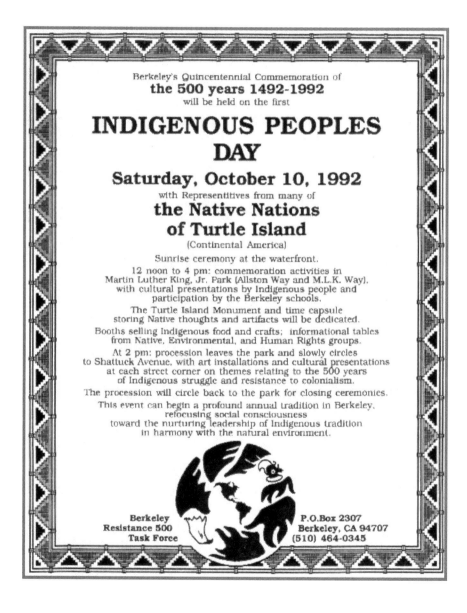

Berkeley
Resistance 500
Task Force

P.O.Box 2307
Berkeley, CA 94707
(510) 464-0345

Procession and Indigenous Peoples Parade

The idea of the Procession was to bring Indigenous Peoples Day downtown into the heart of Berkeley. Shattuck Avenue is the main drag of downtown Berkeley, and MLK, Jr Civic Center Park is behind city hall. The City agreed to close three blocks of the main drag between 2 and 4 pm. It was a moving cultural festival, with music, speakers, poetry, street theatre, informational tables and crafts booths. The procession left the park, walked to Shattuck, and continued down the blocks, stopping for each event, until we reached the Main Library, where we circled back to the park for closing ceremonies.

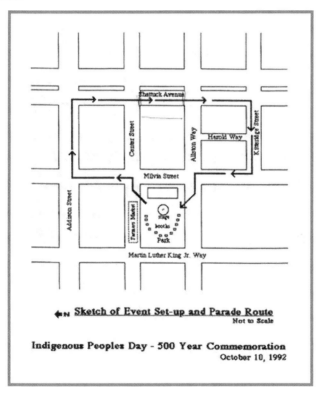

Sketch of Event Set-up and Parade Route
Not to Scale

Indigenous Peoples Day - 500 Year Commemoration
October 10, 1992

The concept of the Procession and Indigenous Peoples Parade came from the Chasky, an annual street event at that time in San Francisco's Mission District, with similar Indigenous themes based on the 500 years. The Chasky had been initiated two years previously, with the participation of some of our committee members, and was part of our Resistance 500 coalition. (See pages 66-70.)

23

Participants in the First Procession

Included in the Berkeley Procession and Tabling were Grupo Maya Kusmej Junan, Antenna Theater, Without Reserve, Earth Circus, Pearl Ubungen Dancers, Musicians Yahuar Wauky, Ingor Gaup, Mahal, Will Knapp, Big Mountain Support Group, Guatemala News and Information Center, PEN Oakland, AWAIR, Roots Against War, Middle East Children's Alliance, Western Shoshone (100th Monkey), Rainforest Action Network, Alliance for Cultural Democracy, Ecology Center, Sarah James' Alaskan Native group, Chicano Human Rights Council, Berkeley Citizens Action, Earth Island Institute, Sister City El Salvador, Oyate, Ecumenical Peace Institute, Real Magic, Cop Watch, Bay Area Landwatch, Labor Committee on the Middle East, and Heyday Books/News from Native California.

Speaking on Shattuck Avenue were Millie Ketcheshawno, Gabriel Hernandez, Lee Sprague, Dennis Jennings, Roberto García, and Mark Gorrell. Poets reading their work were Odelia Rodriguez, Dennis Jennings, Sheila Medina, Floyd Salas, and John Curl.

After the Procession

At Inter-Tribal Friendship House (IFH) and Clinton Park in Oakland, the Bay Area Regional Indian Alliance was simultaneously holding a 1st Nations Inter-Tribal Gathering, with the theme, "Truth In History". At the end of the Berkeley Procession and Indigenous Peoples Parade, the elders and dignitaries who had participated in the Turtle Island dedication, boarded waiting vehicles and drove in a Motorcade to IFH, where a reception for them took place at 4 pm.

TRUTH IN HISTORY
1st Nations InterTribal Gathering

Saturday, October 10, 1992

12 Noon to Sundown
Inter-Tribal Friendship House & Nearby Clinton Park
6th Avenue and E. 14th Street

Please join us on Ohlone Tribal Land to bring our strength and cultural integrity together for:

. Native Music
. Orators
. Arts & Crafts Booths
. Authentic Native American Food
. Large Memorial Participation Painting
. Indian Face Painting
. Finger Painting
. Exhibits on Indian Education, history, tribal law, government,
    health & child welfare

1992 Bay Area Regional Indian Alliance

500 Years of Survival

A reception for the Indian Nations representative to the Berkeley Turtle Island monument dedication will be at 4PM.

The rest of us returned to Martin Luther King, Jr Civic Center Park, where we held closing ceremonies.

As our first Indigenous Peoples Day had begun at sunrise, so it ended at sunset.

[Photos by Nancy Gorrell]

The 1992 sunrise ceremony, presided over by Galeson EagleStar, took place on a hill at Cesar Chavez Park at the Berkeley waterfront.

28

The dedication of the Turtle Island Monument at the first Berkeley Indigenous Peoples Day, led by Dennis Jennings and Mayor Loni Hancock:

[Photos by Nancy Gorrell] [3]

30

20 Years Later

Origins of Indigenous Peoples Day
Excerpts of a Conversation between
Dennis Jennings and John Curl
in 2012[4]

Dennis Jennings was a founder of Berkeley Indigenous Peoples Day, our first coordinator, and Head Man Dancer at the 20th anniversary pow wow of 2012. A member of the Sac and Fox Nation of Oklahoma, he returned to his homeland in the mid-1990s, where he has lived since.

•

JC: Dennis, I'd like to ask you a few questions about Indigenous Peoples Day, your participation in making it happen back then, and what you think of it now 20 years later.

DJ: My memory of 1990-1991 and Indigenous Peoples' Day is all about the thirty to thirty five Indian organizations around the Bay Area. Out of thousands of Indians in the Bay Area, there were only a few dozen of us who had been thinking about this for a decade. My memory goes to Betty Cooper, chairperson of the Bay Area American Indian Alliance, a loose coalition of Indian organizations, mostly government-funded agencies concerned with the social welfare of Native peoples. Betty Cooper was progressive and far thinking, an Alcatraz veteran from the 1960s. Betty recruited and stood firmly behind Millie Ketcheshawno.

JC: Millie was Head Woman Dancer of ourr first pow wow in 1993, and later our coordinator for five years. And of course, her daughter, Leslie Deer, is our Head Lady Dancer this year, and her son, Gino, is now our pow wow coordinator.

DJ: Millie was an organizer of first order. She herself talked about how she had come out of Oklahoma on the government sponsored relocation program, how she arrived on the train with no support services. All those Native Peoples who had been removed and depopulated from their own homelands in the 1950s had arrived in various big cities with no support services, no community organizations. Betty and Millie and my own Wahpepah relatives had fought tooth and nail for services away from the land, for help with training and jobs and employment and health and school books and clothes. Now it was that thirty plus Native American organizations could have an alliance after decades of organizing and fighting for their rights. Betty said at least once in those days that Dennis was my left hand and Fred Short was my right hand. To me it was Betty Cooper who sent us to Berkeley.

JC: I didn't really know Betty. I heard that the Bay Area Indian Alliance was holding a conference at DQ University near Davis, and when they moved the conference to Laney College on its last day and opened it to non-Native people, I and a lot of other nonIndians joined in. I brought Mark and Nancy Gorrell to that conference, whom I knew from local politics, BCA. I believe that was also the first time I met you, as well as Lee Sprague and many other people. And out of that we organized the Berkeley chapter of Resistance 500. Our group became an official City task force with the mission of reporting on what the City should do for the Quincentennial.

DJ: In the rest of the Bay Area there was a lot of confusion and chaos about how to proceed, but there appeared in Berkeley an organized group of people who genuinely wanted to accept some ideas of what could be done with the old worn out concept of Columbus Day. To my knowledge, this was an outgrowth of the Berkeley Citizens' Action. They had even sent a representative to Quito, Ecuador to the meeting of all meetings on the whole continent to discuss this question. Personally I did not go to Ecuador, but I had helped raise money and make decisions on who should go and how to make decisions on who should go. It was in Quito that a multinational decision was made to change Cristobal Colon Day into Indigenous Peoples Day. In Berkeley we met non-Indians who did not have to be taught this concept. We met and appreciated political people who were experienced, brainy, down to earth, and organized.

JC: Actually, I was the representative who went to Quito. Here's how it happened. In 1990 was receiving a little newsletter from the South

American Indian Information Center, which was run out of Oakland by Nilo Cayuqueo, a Mapuche man from Chile. In the newsletter was a small notice about the upcoming conference in Ecuador. I went down to the Oakland office and explained to Nilo that I was interested in getting involved with counter-quincentennial activities locally. Together he and I came up with the idea that I would go to the Berkeley mayor, Loni Hancock, whom I knew from working on her election campaigns, and ask her to send me to the conference as her representative, to gather information about how Berkeley should commemorate the quincentennial. I would pay for everything myself. And that is what happened. When I got back, we had a meeting of Loni, Nilo, and Tony Gonzales of the International Indian Treaty Council. Tony brought Millie Ketcheshawno to the meeting. That was the first time I met Millie.

DJ: After much planning and after the decision of the City Council, we were prepared to work! What really helped is that Millie and the Mayor Loni Hancock seemed to me not just on the same page but like good friends. Because of Millie and Betty and the Berkeley Committee, I got to work in City Hall, an office overlooking the park for several weeks. My memories of those fast moving days and weeks in 1991 and 1992 are now a haze with brilliant flashes of highpoints jumping out. I know that much argument and debate preceded our primary slogan, our preeminent concept, "Tell the children the truth!"

JC: Right, we studied the true history for a long time, debated it, then went back to the city council again and presented research showing how Columbus sent shiploads of enslaved Indians back to Spain, and invented the transatlantic slave trade. Under Columbus's leadership, over a hundred thousand Taino Indians on the island of Hispanola were killed and the survivors were enslaved in mines and plantations. So the task force proposed to the City Council to replace Columbus Day with Indigenous Peoples Day. And in October, 1991, that is what they did, unanimously.

DJ: We knew we did not just want one day to do this so we planned for the whole year. We worked on exhibits for all the public and private galleries of art for the visual public aspect of anticipation. We had school programs in various local schools to promote reading about the true history of this land. Some of us were contracted to work on exhibits in the Livermore Museum, which were then copied and shipped to six other major educational museums elsewhere, including the Smithsonian. A group of us with the help of a Berkeley resident and professional theater artists, produced a play from oral histories available to us from UC about a fishing struggle case that twenty years earlier had gone to the US Supreme court. Many other efforts occurred far and wide. I promoted a public speaking activity called "Soapbox-Chautauqua," which I recorded and edited and put on KPFA. I am very thankful that I got to work in and for the City of Berkeley and for my brand of people.

JC: And now it's twenty years later. Of course, besides the 20th anniversary of Indigenous Peoples Day, this is also the 520th anniversary of Indigenous resistance and survival in the face of European colonialism.

DJ: I am exceptionally proud that twenty years later somebody remembered me well enough to ask me to come back and be a Head Dancer in an activity that I had but a small part in starting.

•

Treaty Council
Indigenous Peoples Day Sunrise Ceremony
on Alcatraz Island

On October 12, 1991, ten days before Berkeley made Indigenous Peoples Day an official city holiday, the International Indian Treaty Council (IITC) held the first Indigenous Peoples Day sunrise ceremony on Alcatraz Island. The Treaty Council and our Berkeley committee had been working closely together for the previous six months in the Resistance 500 coalition.

Organized by Antonio Gonzales and many others, the Treaty Council ferried around 300 people from San Francisco to Alcatraz island, where we celebrated at the ceremonial fire. Since this is Ohlone land, representatives of that nation served as host and welcomed us.

Activist Willie Lonewolf, center, joins in song and drums during a sunrise ceremony yesterday on Alcatraz Island.

[*Oakland Tribune* 10/13/92]

The 1969 occupation of Alcatraz island and the deserted prison by Indians of All Tribes, led by a group of Native college students, was the spark that reignited North American Indian activism and the catalyst for many profound and permanent changes. The occupation

36

was instrumental in transforming how Native people saw their culture, rights, and identity; it helped to change the relationship between Native and non-Native people in the US; and led to the transformation of the federal government's policy from genocidal "termination" to Indian self-determination. The importance of the Alcatraz occupation cannot be overstated. We in Berkeley Resistance 500 were most deeply honored that Millie Ketcheshawno, Dennis Jennings, and others involved with the original occupation were now participating closely in our project.

To commemorate the Alcatraz occupation, the Treaty Council first began the annual tradition in 1975 of a sunrise ceremony on the island every Unthanksgiving Day. Millie Ketcheshawno was among the many who helped initiate the Unthanksgiving sunrise gathering. This was two years before Indigenous Peoples Day was first conceived.

The Treaty Council has been involved with Indigenous Peoples Day starting from its very first conception. They were instrumental .in the historic United Nations Geneva Indigenous Conference that put out the original call for Indigenous Peoples Day in 1977. Treaty Council members participated in the Quito Encuentro of 1990. They were part of BARIA and Resistance 500, the coalitions organizing the Bay Area Counter-Quincentenary in 1991-92.

For more about the Treaty Council's contributions to Indigenous Peoples Day, see pages 74 and 104.

1992: A Year of Indigenous Events

Indigenous Peoples Day 1992 was not a one-day event, but the culmination of an entire year of related events in Berkeley and around the Bay Area.

Berkeley School Board

Soon after the City Council enacted Indigenous Peoples Day, the Berkeley School Board added their support of a year of educational activities in the schools.

Item #10
11/20/91

RESOLUTION NO. 4960

**BERKELEY UNIFIED SCHOOL DISTRICT
BOARD OF EDUCATION ACKNOWLEDGES
1992 AS THE YEAR OF THE INDIGENOUS PEOPLE**

WHEREAS, the Berkeley Unified School District recognizes October 12, 1992 as a day to recognize the culture and contribution of Indigenous People; and

WHEREAS, the public schools in Berkeley, K-12, will include during the 1992 school year classroom discussions and projects regarding the history of the Indigenous People; and

WHEREAS, the students in the Berkeley Unified School District will be encouraged to attend cultural events and films at the Pacific Film Archives relating to Indigenous People; and

WHEREAS, students in the Berkeley Unified School District will be encouraged to participate in a poster contest celebrating the year of the Indigenous People; and

WHEREAS, students in the Berkeley Unified School District will be encouraged to attend the exhibit entitled *1492: Two Worlds of Science* at the Lawrence Hall of Science at the University of California, Berkeley, between October 12, 1991 and January 5, 1992;

NOW, THEREFORE, BE IT RESOLVED that the Board of Education of the Berkeley Unified School District will encourage participation in the above mentioned activities regarding the year 1992 being declared the Year of the Indigenous People.

PASSED AND ADOPTED by the Board of Education of the Berkeley Unified School District this 20th day of November, 1991, by the following called vote:

AYES: Directors Acevedo, Hegarty, Noguera, Shaughnessy, Topel, (Dorman)

NOES: None

ABSENT: None

ABSTAIN: None

LaVoncia C. Steele. Ed.D.
Secretary of the Board of Education
of the City of Berkeley and of the
Berkeley Unified School District of
Alameda County, State of California

Berkeley Public Library Exhibition

We set up an exhibit in the front windows of the downtown Berkeley library, and other exhibits in glass display cases inside the ground floor entrance way, that opened in January, 1992.

Mayor Loni organized a press conference in front of the library at the opening of the exhibit, with Dennis, herself, and the heads of the school board and the library. The press came out in force.

[Photo by John Curl]
Dennis Jennings and Loni Hancock at the press conference

39

We continued organizing for community consciousness of a year of activities, focused on October, 1992.

Berkeley RESISTANCE 500

PO Box 2307, Berkeley, CA 94702 • (510) 464-3045

1992 the Year of Indigenous People in Berkeley

The City Council has proclaimed that 1992 will be commemorated in Berkeley as the Year of Indigenous People, and October 12th will henceforth no longer be "Columbus Day," but the Day of Solidarity with Indigenous People.

The Berkeley Resistance 500 Task Force, set up by the City Council, is working with the City, the Public Libraries, the School System, community organizations and city commissions to implement year-long activities.

The Berkeley School Board has resolved to stress the history and issues of the 500 years during the 1992 school year, including classroom discussions and special projects. The Task Force will be working with them to institute in-service teacher training and permanently change the place of Native Americans in the school curriculum.

The Task Force is working with the library to improve their collection on Native people and the European invasion of the Americas, offering critiques of existing literature and consultation on obtaining new books, videos, records, and Indigenous periodicals.

The Task Force will be preparing public displays on different themes in the entrance to the Main Library and at other locations. The first display will begin on December 31, 1991 on the theme of Treaties, issues of sovereignty of the Native Nations and the debt of the US Constitution to the Great Law of the Hau De No Sau Nee (Iroquois).

The Council called on newspapers, radio and cable stations to issue regular reminders throughout the year of Indigenous issues and events.

Berkeley is beginning preparations for the Quincentennial commemoration of October 1992, which we envision to be a major event on the weekend before the 12th, drawing in much of the Berkeley community. It will include ceremonies, cultural events and speakers, with participation from the schools. The Council agreed to sponsor. by providing space and assistance. a monument dedicated to the Indigenous Peoples impacted by the Columbus-led invasion. The monument may include a time capsule storing Native thoughts and artifacts for future generations. The dedication of this monument may take place as part of the October 1992 commemoration activities.

The City Council called on the University of California Anthropology Department to complete its returning of all bones of Indigenous people to conform with the Native American Graves and Repatriation Act of 1990; and encouraged the University to establish a "think tank" to assist Indian struggles. The Task Force will be working to implement this resolution.

Finally, the Council encouraged the people of Berkeley to reach out in solidarity with Indigenous peoples around the world and their struggles.

If you want to work on any of these projects, want information on upcoming meetings, or want to connect us with other projects of your own, please contact us.

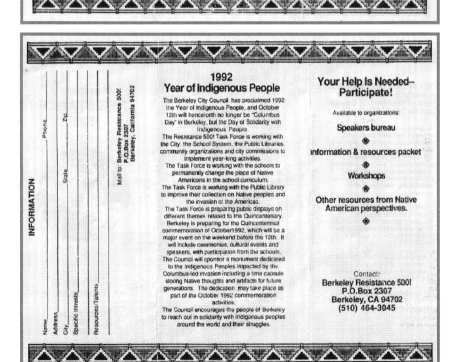

The Berkeley Resistance 500! Task Force was set up as a joint effort of the City Council and the School Board:

"to develop, recommend and implement activities for the 500th anniversary of Columbus' first voyage that conform to the Berkeley Human Rights Ordinance, the U.N. Charter, and the civil liberties guarantees in the California constitution by presenting an alternative view to the traditional presentations of this event in ways that will involve and inform the community...

"The traditional and historic perspective on this event has been exclusively Eurocentric: ignoring the brutal realities of the subjugation and colonization of the indigenous peoples this expedition encountered.

"Community activities can be dedicated to an accurate history, recognition and celebration of our diversity, and learning from history rather than repeating it.

"All the residents of Berkeley of every heritage will benefit from such an alternative view."

Berkeley Resistance 500!
is part of

Resistance 500!

"an alliance of indigenous people and people of the four sacred colors to express our true history of resistance against 500 years of colonialism."

Both our Berkeley group and the Bay Area-wide coalition hold monthly meetings to coordinate activities and actions related to the 500-years campaign.

Contact us for further information about up and coming meetings

Berkeley Resistance 500!
P.O.Box 2307
Berkeley, CA 94702
(510) 464-3045

Berkeley RESISTANCE 500!

500 Years of Resistance

Organizing for
1992
and beyond

1992
Year of Indigenous People

The Berkeley City Council has proclaimed 1992 the Year of Indigenous People, and October 12th will henceforth no longer be "Columbus Day" in Berkeley, but the Day of Solidarity with Indigenous People.

The Resistance 500! Task Force is working with the City, the School System, the Public Libraries, community organizations and city commissions to implement year-long activities.

The Task Force is working with the schools to permanently change the place of Native Americans in the school curriculum.

The Task Force is working with the Public Library to improve their collection on Native peoples and the invasion of the Americas.

The Task Force is preparing public displays on different themes related to the Quincentenary.

Berkeley is preparing for the Quincentennial commemoration of October 1992, which will be a major event on the weekend before the 12th. It will include ceremonies, cultural events and speakers, with participation from the schools.

The Council will sponsor a monument dedicated to the Indigenous Peoples impacted by the Columbus-led invasion including a time capsule storing Native thoughts and artifacts for future generations. The dedication may take place as part of the October 1992 commemoration activities.

The Council encourages the people of Berkeley to reach out in solidarity with indigenous peoples around the world and their struggles.

Your Help Is Needed— Participate!

Available to organizations:

Speakers bureau

❀

Information & resources packet

❀

Workshops

❀

Other resources from Native American perspectives.

❀

Contact:
Berkeley Resistance 500!
P.O.Box 2307
Berkeley, CA 94702
(510) 464-3045

INFORMATION

Name

Address

City _____ State _____ Zip _____

Phone

Specific interests

Resources/Talents

Mail to: Berkeley Resistance 500!
P.O.Box 2307
Berkeley, California 94702

Mayor Hancock continued to give us her active support.

Berkeley Mayor Loni Hancock, fourth from left, receives a plaque on behalf of American Indians nationwide from Dennis Banks. Darrell Standing Elk, Millie Ketcheshawno, John LaVelle and Floyd 'Red Crow' Westerman.

By Wendy Lamm/Oakland Tribune

[SF Chronicle 3/7/92]

Loni Hancock receives an honor from Dennis Banks,
Darrell Standing Elk, Millie Ketcheshawno,
John La Velle, & Floyd 'Red Crow' Westerman.

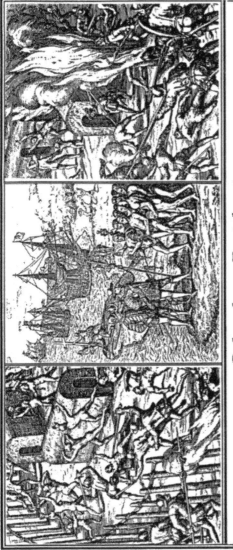

Columbus Factsheet

- At the very first Caribbean island where he landed Columbus kidnapped six Taíno Indians.

- He came in search of gold and power. He thought he was near Asia and made plans to conquer the continent.

- The Caribbean Islands were populated by 1 to 4 million Taíno Indians, a peaceful nation.

- Unable to find enough gold to finance his schemes, Columbus captured thousands of Taínos and shipped them to the slave markets of Spain. The Taínos resisted with fishbone-tipped spears, but these were no match for artillery. Columbus demanded that each adult Taíno pay a tribute of gold every three months, under penalty of amputation of the hands. Many fled to the mountains but Columbus' men tracked them down with dogs. Rather than be slaves, thousands took poison. In two years over a hundred thousand Taínos were dead, and the survivors were slaves in the mines and plantations. Within two decades the genocide of the Taíno nation was complete, and the Spaniards began importing slaves from Africa.

- Columbus was unrepentantly guilty of the genocide of over two million Indian people.

- Columbus invented European imperialism in the Americas and the transatlantic slave trade.

- At the quincentennial of the Columbus invasion, let us rediscover the true history of our hemisphere, and celebrate the 500 years of resistance and survival of all Indigenous peoples against colonialism and imperialism.

Berkeley Resistance 900 Task Force • Indigenous People Day Committee
P.O. Box 2307 Berkeley, CA 94710 • (510) 548-1992

Resistance 500!
Organizing for 1992 & Beyond

PO Box 2307, Berkeley, CA 94702
(510) 464-3045

September 16, 1992

Hello friends,

We are writing to request your participation on Indigenous Peoples Day, Saturday, October 10, 1992. The day will be filled with cultural and ceremonial activities. Elders and emissaries of many Native Nations will be in attendance at Berkeley's Martin Luther King, Jr. Park (Allston Way & MLK). The day will begin with a dedication and groundbreaking ceremonies for the Turtle Island Monument and time capsule, which will be erected behind Berkeley City Hall inside of the Peace Wall. The monument is intended to focus attention on the struggles of Indigenous Peoples all over Mother Earth in their continued resistance to this resource mongering modern society, to honor the memory of those Native Nations and their patriots and Martyrs long gone, and to acknowledge the contribution of the precolumbian cultures to our modern world.

After the dedication many of the Indigenous delegates will be transported to the Inter-Tribal Friendship House at 14th Street and 5th Avenue in Oakland where they will be guests of the local native American community at an activity sponsored by the 1992 Bay Area Indian Alliance. During this time the Berkeley crowd will form a procession to Shattuck Avenue for cultural presentations on themes of the resistance.

Please notify all of your friends, neighbors, colleagues, and members of your organization and encourage them to participate in these activities. Posters and flyers will be posted in various places around Berkeley to call attention to the event. You are encouraged to set up a table to distribute information or sell materials. The requisite form is on the back of this letter.

If you would like to help with logistics, publicity, distribution of flyers and posters or if you are willing to help with security for the event itself, please call (510) 548-1992.

We look forward to seeing you on the 10th.

Dennis Jennings
Coordinator, Indigenous Peoples Day
Berkeley Resistance 500 Task Force
(510) 548-1992

John Curl
Procession and Tabling Coordinator
Berkeley Indigenous People's Day Committee
(510) 420-1015, (510) 548-1992

Turtle Island Monument

PETER DA SILVA — Staff

Lee A. Sprague, left, primary architect of the Turtle Island Project, watches as vernal equinox celebrants stand eggs on their ends.

Solar studies start for Indian Monument

[*Oakland Tribune*, March 22, 1994]

Lee Sprague's concept of the Turtle Island Monument took on a life of its own and had a separate trajectory through the city processes. As public art and a proposed structure in Civic Center ML King, Jr. Park, it needed to pass through the Public Arts Commission and other agencies related to the parks. Lee always projected the rightness and purity of his vision, so many people became supporters.

The dedication of the Turtle Island Monument was a centerpiece of the events of the first Berkeley Indigenous Peoples Day.

Lee was confident that once the city approved the concept, funds to build it could be gathered from outside sources. So at this time the cost of the project to the city was never an issue. Besides, the old fountain in the park, originally built in the 1930s, had been broken for as long as anyone could remember, and most people saw it as an eyesore. So at that time nobody objected to replacing it with the Turtle Island Monument.

The mayor's office sent out this press release for the Turtle Island Monument dedication ceremonies:

CITY OF BERKELEY

FOR IMMEDIATE RELEASE

Loni Hancock
MAYOR

October 8, 1992, Berkeley, California
Contact: A.Robin Orden, Office of the Mayor   510/644-6484
            Dennis Jennings, Indigenous Peoples Day Cte 510/548-1992

BERKELEY DEDICATES TURTLE ISLAND MONUMENT AS PART OF INDIGENOUS PEOPLES DAY ACTIVITIES

On Saturday October 10th, 1992 the City of Berkeley will host an outdoor program as part of its first Indigenous Peoples Day activities. The program runs from 10:00 a.m. until 2:00 p.m. in Martin Luther King, Jr. Park with acoustic music and a variety of cultural events. At 2:00, the commemoration will move to the BART Plaza at Shattuck Avenue and Center Street for a continuation of cultural activities until 4:00 pm.

The highlight of the day's events will be the dedication of the site for the Turtle Island Monument from 11:00 until 1:00. The Monument will honor the Native People of this hemisphere, whose societies flourished centuries before Columbus arrived and which continue on this day. 1992 is seen as the end of 500 years of resistance and the beginning of 500 years of rebuilding by the Indigenous People of Turtle Island. Among those expected at the dedication are leaders and elders of many Native Peoples, including the Ohlone of our area in California.

In dedicating the Monument, Mayor Loni Hancock recognized "the care that Native People have had for this land long before Columbus and in honor of their culture and philosophy, which are needed now more than ever if the planet is to survive".

- # -

Martin Luther King, Jr. Civic Center   2180 Milvia Street   Berkeley, California 94704

Telephone(510) 644-6484
TDD (510) 644-8678

•

46

Almost every Native nation and tribe tells a version of the creation history of Turtle Island. This is Lee Sprague's telling of the story according to the Potawatomi:

~~~~~~~~~~~~~~~~~~~~~~~~~~~~

The Creation of Turtle Island
By Lee Sprague

In my people's creation stories the world was covered with water and all the animals were swimming.

They were getting tired, so they respectfully asked the muskrat to go under the water to see if there was any earth. So the muskrat went down to find the earth. All of the animals were waiting for the muskrat to reappear. They were worried for the muskrat. Finally his body floated to the surface. The animals looked in his paw and they found some earth. They put the earth on the turtle's back.

The rest of the animals now knew that there was earth under the water so they each went down to get some earth, first the loon then the duck and all of the rest of the animals. They all put the Earth on the turtle's back. This Is how Turtle Island was created.[5]

See Appendix A, on page 153 for the further history of the Turtle Island fountain.

•

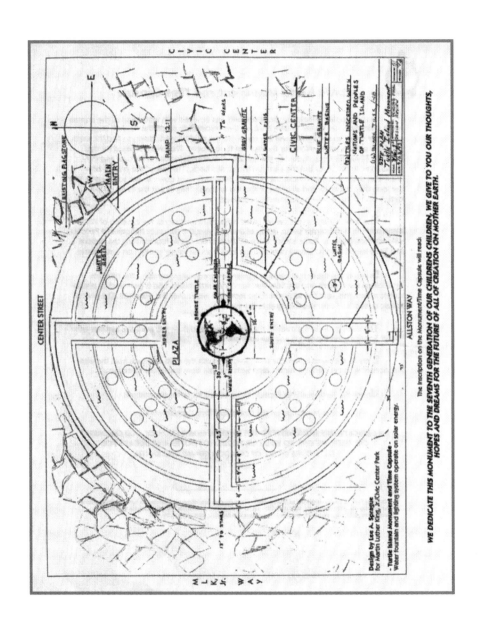

CIVIC CENTER

CENTER STREET

ALLSTON WAY

EXISTING FLAGSTONE

MAIN ENTRY

RAMP 12:1

GRAY GRANITE

WATER POOL

CIVIC CENTER

BLUE GRANITE
WATER BASIN

DETAILS INSCRIBED WITH NATIONS AND PEOPLES OF TURTLE ISLAND

PLAZA

BRONZE TURTLE

WATER BASIN

SOUTH ENTRY

WATER GARDEN

Design by Lee A. Sprague
for Martin Luther King, Jr./Civic Center Park

- Turtle Island Monument and Time Capsule -
Water fountain and lighting system operate on solar energy.

The inscription on the Monument/Time Capsule will read:

WE DEDICATE THIS MONUMENT TO THE SEVENTH GENERATION OF OUR CHILDRENS CHILDREN; WE GIVE TO YOU OUR THOUGHTS, HOPES AND DREAMS FOR THE FUTURE OF ALL OF CREATION ON MOTHER EARTH.

MLK Jr. Way

Cultural Festival of Poetry and Music
Celebrating 500 Years of Resistance

On May 27, we put on a Cultural Festival of Poetry and Music at La Peña Cultural Center with fifteen poets.

Resistance 500 Coalition and La Peña Cultural Center Present

A Gathering of Many Voices
Celebrating 500 Years of Resistance
A Cultural Festival of Poetry and Music with

Francisco X Alarcón

Katia Aparicio

Jose Antonio Burciaga

John Curl

Jack Foley

Samuel Guia

Lakota Hardin

Barbara Jameson

Dennis Jennings

Sheila Medina

Jose Montoya

Mary Rudge

Floyd Salas

Piri Thomas

Fernando Torres

Songs by Lichi Fuentes

Wednesday • May 27 • 1992 • 7:30pm • $3-5

La Peña Cultural Center 3105 Shattuck Ave. Berkeley

510-849-2568 One Block East Of Ashby Bart Station/Benefiting the Resistance 500 Coalition

Multi-Cultural Book Fair

On May 30 we organized a Multi-Cultural Book Fair at the gym at Berkeley High School, with nineteen vendors, author book signings, poster sessions, storytelling, all day video showings. The R500 Education Committee, made up of Roberto José García, Gabriel Hernandez, Nancy Schimmel, Audrey Shabbas, and Jennifer Smith, were the central organizers.

6 TUESDAY, JANUARY 14, 1992 THE DAILY CALIFORNIAN

Jose Garcia, a member of Resistance 500, displays books depicting Native Americans with a non-traditional historical perspective.

[Daily Californian, 1/14/92]
Roberto José García at the Book Fair

Resistance 500!
Organizing for 1992 & Beyond

PO Box 2387, Berkeley, CA 94782
(510) 464-3845

The City of Berkeley's
Resistance 500 Taskforce
invites you to a

Multi-Cultural Book Fair

Saturday, May 30, 1992
10:00 a.m. – 4:00 p.m.
Berkeley High School
SMALL GYMNASIUM

This will be an outstanding opportunity to examine the issues, explore promising practices, network with others, and become aware of resources to assist us in the celebration of our diversity.

There will be exhibits of books and materials representing all cultural and ethnic groups.

There will be continuous showings of video resources on the theme of "Resistance 500."

There will also be posters sessions providing the opportunity to meet teachers who have developed marvelous classroom lessons as they relate to the Columbus "discovery" and its consequences for the indigenous peoples of the Americas.

The focus of the Book Fair will be global cultural and linguistic diversity. This will be a marvelous opportunity to examine student materials, teacher background materials, literature, media, and software.

All of the residents of the Bay Area of every heritage will benefit from this very special day!

For further information about the day's events
(510) 704-0517.

51

UCB Lawrence Hall of Science Exhibition

We worked on the University of California's Berkeley Lawrence Hall of Science exhibition "1492: Two Worlds of Science," which ran between October, 1991 until January, 1992. They hired Lee Sprague as a consultant. With Lee's assistance, the result focused on many of the core issues. As a newspaper article at the time described, "The exhibits use science to address painful aspects of history, such as slavery, genocide and ecological destruction, that often have been overlooked in discussions of Columbus's exploration."

BY EDDIE LEDESMA/THE CHRONICLE

Lee Sprague, exhibit consultant, said it is 'time to reexamine the history of the impact of Columbus on native peoples'

[*SF Chronicle* 10/10/91]
Lee Sprague at the Lawrence Hall of Science exhibit.

Soapbox-Chautauqua

On July 29 we organized a Soapbox-Chautauqua at the Berkeley Unitarian Fellowship Hall, an open mike on quincentennial issues, a forum where people of different backgrounds stepped up one by one and spoke from the heart about Indigenous Peoples Day. We did another Chautauqua on September 17.

Was He A Fool?

We sponsored and some of us actually acted in a satirical play about Columbus at nearby Mills College.

Resistance 500

In 1992, the Resistance 500 coalition had at least 85 affiliated groups, and each group organized events.

A Bay Area Resistance 500 Directory

July 21, 1992

1992 Committee, Santa Cruz   POBox 160328, Santa Cruz, CA 95063 (408) 427-4533
500 Years Coalition, Santa Clara Valley   POBox 160328, Cupertino, CA 95015-0328
All People's Congress   2489 Mission Street #28 (at 21st), San Francisco, CA 94110 (415) 821-6545
Alliance for Cultural Democracy   1340 Peralta Avenue, Berkeley, CA 94702
Amazonia Voices of the Rainforest, The   POBox 77438, San Francisco, CA 94107 (415) 243-4146 fax (415) 243-0661
American Indian AIDS Institute of San Francisco   333 Valencia Street #200, San Francisco, CA 94103 (415) 626-7639
American Indian Alliance   Humboldt State University, Arcata, CA 95521
American Indian Center Library   919 The Alameda, San Jose, CA 94912 (408) 971-9622
American Indian Contemporary Arts   685 Market Street, San Francisco, CA 94105 (415) 495-7600
American Indian Film Institute   333 Valencia Street #322, San Francisco, CA 94103 (415) 554-0525
American Indian Graduate Department   University of California, Berkeley, 140 Warren Hall, Berkeley, CA 94720
American Indian Movement (AIM)   2940 16th st #104, San Francisco, CA 94103 (415) 552-1992
American Indian Studies   San Francisco State University, 1600 Holloway Avenue, San Francisco, CA 94132
Ashkenaz Music and Dance Cafe   1317 San Pablo Avenue, Berkeley, CA 94702 (510) 525-5054
Aztlan Cultural: Centro Chicano / Latino De Escritores   131 Stephen Street, Santa Cruz, CA 95060 (408) 423-6308; (408) 459-4079
Bay Area Indian Agency Representatives   c/o Intertribal Friendship House, 523 East 14th Street, Oakland, CA 94606 (510) 452-1235 fax (510) 452-1243
Bay Area Regional Indian Alliance   c/o Intertribal Friendship House, 523 East 14th Street, Oakland, CA 94606 (510) 452-1235
Big Mountain Support Group   POBox 882221, San Francisco, CA 94188-2221 (415) 821-9157
Big Picture Productions   2215-R Market #464, San Francisco, CA 94114 (415) 995-4685
Campus Activist Alliance, Bay Area (BACAA)   130 Bryant, Palo Alto, CA 94301 (415) 328-2367
Center for the Support and Protection of Indian Religions and Indigenous Traditions (SPIRIT)   POBox 17002, Oakland, CA 94601 (510) 535-0505
Central American Mission Partners (CAMP)   POBox 10206, Oakland, CA 94610 (510) 644-2207 fax (510) 849-4082
Central Coast Quincentennial Indian Council   226 Younglove Avenue, Santa Cruz, CA 95060
Cherky   3311 Mission Street #171, San Francisco, CA 94110 (415) 885-4749 (Life on the Water)
Chicano Moratorium Coalition   POBox 2031, Berkeley, CA 94702-0031 (510) 893-3181; (510) 581-4566 fax (510) 893-3362
DQ University   2021 P Street, Sacramento, CA 95814
Earth Action Network   1711-D MLKing Way, Berkeley, CA 94709 (510) 843-4306 fax (510) 649-1895
Earth First!, Bay Area   POBox 411233, San Francisco, CA 94141 (415) 949-0575 (event hotline)
Ecology Center   2530 San Pablo Avenue (near Dwight Way), Berkeley, CA 94702 (510) 548-2220; (510) 644-3822 (recycling hotline)
Food Not Bombs, San Francisco   3145 Geary Blvd. #12, San Francisco, CA 94118 (415) 330-5030
Gathering Tribes Gallery   1308-F Solano Avenue, Albany, CA 94706 (510) 528-9038
Global Anti-Nuclear Alliance   c/o Western States Legal Foundation, 1440 Broadway #500, Oakland, CA 94612 (510) 839-5877
Global Exchange   2141 Mission Street #202, San Francisco, CA 94110 (415) 255-7296; (415) 648-8068 (SF store); (510) 548-0370 (Berkeley store)
Green Party, Bay Area   POBox 20999, Oakland, CA 94620 (510) 549-9993
Hitec Aztec Productions   3500 Clayton Road #B-232, Concord, CA 94519 (510) 687-9655 fax (510) 689-0179
Indian Historian Press   1493 Masonic Avenue, San Francisco, CA 94117
Indigenous Women's Network   546 30th Street, San Francisco, CA 94119
Inter-Tribal Council of California   2021 P Street, Sacramento, CA 95814
International Campaign to Free geronimo ji Jaga (Pratt)   POBox 3585, Oakland, CA 94609-0585 (510) 268-0979; (510) 655-2587; (510) 486-8224
International Indian Treaty Council (IITC)   710 Clayton Street #1, San Francisco, CA 94117 (415) 566-0251 fax (415) 566-0442
International Tribunal Office   2940 16th st #104, San Francisco, CA 94103 (415) 552-1992
Intertribal Friendship House   523 East 14th Street, Oakland, CA 94606 (510) 452-1235
John Brown Anti-Klan Committee   220 Ninth Street #443, San Francisco, CA 94103 (415) 330-5363
Komotion International   POBox 410502, San Francisco, CA 94141-0502 (415) 646-4923
La Pena Cultural Center   3105 Shattuck, Berkeley, CA 94705 (510) 849-2568; (510) 849-2573 (for info on events) fax (510) 849-9397
Leonard Peltier Support Group   2940 16th st #104, San Francisco, CA 94103 (415) 552-1992
Life On the Water   Fort Mason, Bldg. B, San Francisco, CA 94123 (415) 885-2790 (office); (415) 885-4749 (Quincentenary); fax (415) 885-4257
Little Moon, Matt   762 15th Street #8, Oakland, CA 94612-1066 (510) 632-5052
Living Fire / Eagle Jaguar Clan   2859 Hermosa Street, Pinole, CA 94564-1511 (510) 223-0357
Living Spirit   POBox 160328, Cupertino, CA 94702 (408) 253-5000
National Chicano Human Rights Council   POBox 2551, Berkeley, CA 94702 (510) 893-3181 fax (510) 893-3362
National Network for Immigrant & Refugee Rights (NNIRR)   310 8th Street #307, Oakland, CA 94607 (510) 465-1984
Native American Studies   University of California, Davis, CA 95616 (916) 752-3237 fax (916) 752-5363
New College of California   50 Fell Street, San Francisco, CA 94102 (415) 626-1694
New World Times   625 Ashbury Street #14, San Francisco, CA 94117 (415) 864-0487; (415) 864-3915 fax (415) 864-0455
News from Native California   POBox 9145, Berkeley, CA 94709 (510) 549-3564
Norma Jean Croy Defense Committee (NJCDC)   473 Jackson Street, 3rd Floor, San Francisco, CA 94111 (415) 986-5591
Our Developing World   13004 Paseo Presada, Saratoga, CA 95070 (408) 379-4431
Oyate   2702 Mathews, Berkeley, CA 94702 (510) 848-6700
Paper Tiger TV West / Deep Dish Satellite Network   POBox 1271, San Francisco, CA 94141-1271 (415) 695-0931
Peace and Dignity Journeys 1992   3500 Clayton Road #B-232, Concord, CA 94519 (510) 687-9655; fax (510) 689-0179
Peace Test, Bay Area   POBox 40712, San Francisco, CA 94107 (415) 863-9105
People's Bulletin Board   c/o J.C. Miller, 2100 MLKing Jr. Way, Berkeley, CA 94704
People's Park Defense Union (PPDU)   1901 Sixth Street, Berkeley, CA 94710 (510) 843-6788 (recorded hotline); (510) 843-4306
Pledge of Resistance, Bay Area   4228 Telegraph Avenue, Oakland, CA 94610 (510) 655-1177 (Bay Area chapter); (510) 655-1181 (National)
Prairie Fire Organizing Committee   POBox 14422, San Francisco, CA 94114 (415) 330-5310
Rainforest Action Network (RAN)   450 Sansome Street #700 (at Sansome), San Francisco, CA 94111 (415) 398-4404 fax (415) 398-2732
Redwood Cultural Network   POBox 10408, Oakland, CA 94610 (800) 888-SONG; (510) 835-1445
Resistance 500 Task Force, Berkeley   POBox 2307, Berkeley, CA 94702 (510) 464-3045
Resistance 500!   c/o Intertribal Friendship House, 523 East 14th Street, Oakland, CA 94606 (510) 452-1235 fax (510) 452-1243
Rock Against Racism   1827 Haight Street, Box 57, San Francisco, CA 94117 (415) 267-3171; (510) 665-8114; (510) 841-4105/06
Seeds of Peace   POBox 12154, Oakland, CA 94604 (510) 420-1799 fax (510) 834-3741
Sonoma County Rainbow Greens   POBox 296, Occidental, CA 95465 (707) 829-2417; (707) 874-2248; (707) 545-8426
South and Meso-American Indian Information Center (SAIIC)   POBox 28703, Oakland, CA 94604 (510) 834-4263 fax (510) 834-4264
South Bay Quincentennial Indigenous Council   POBox 160328, Cupertino, CA 95016 (408) 255-2750
South-North Communication Network, The   POBox 410150, San Francisco, CA 94141 (415) 821-8961
Spiritual Walk (1992 and Beyond)   (415) 541-5032 (24-hour voicemail)
Toward a Human Future   266 Madison Street, San Francisco, CA 94134 (415) 586-2217
Turtle Island Project (TIPI)   POBox 40244, Berkeley, CA 94704 (510) 569-2834 (Lee Sprague)
United Against Genocide: 1992   c/o Intertribal Friendship House, 523 East 14th Street, Oakland, CA 94606 (510) 826-1054

As we did our work, so did the other groups in our coalition. Resistance 500 flyers listed 68 Bay Area events between July 22 through October, 1992.

Some Resistance 500 Events

September 15, 1992 01:12 PM

Monthly Planning Meeting of the Resistance 500 Coalition Come help prepare for October's activities [info (510) 452-1235]
Sep 17 (thu) 7:00 pm at the Intertribal Friendship House, 523 East 14th Street (near 5th Avenue) in Oakland

Resistance 500 Soapbox / Chautauqua an open-mike opportunity for you to comment on the invasion of this land 500 years ago
Sep 17 (thu) 7:00 pm at the Unitarian Fellowship Church, Cedar at Bonita in Berkeley [Dennie Jennings (510) 548-1992]

The Panama Deception new film revealing the alarming, untold story of the December 1989 US invasion of Panama
Sep 17 (thu) 7:00 pm benefit reception with the filmmakers; 8:00 pm Michael Parenti & Barbara Trent Speak, then film ($15)
Sep 18 (fri) 7:00 & 9:30 pm; Sep 19 & 20 2:00, 4:30, 7:00 & 9:30 pm film only at UC Theatre, University Av at Shattuck in Berkeley

Environmental Conquest: 1492 to 1992 a forum to benefit AIM's 500 Years of Resistance activities, with Nilak Butler (Inuit, Indigenous Environmental Network / Women's Network), Alejandro Molina (National Committee to Free Puerto Rican Prisoners of War), & Audrey Lawrence (Nindakin: People of Color for the Environment) [American Indian Movement (415) 552-1992] ($3 to $10)
Sep 17 (thu) 7:30 pm at the Women's Building, 3543 18th Street (near Valencia) in SF [Political Ecology Group (415) 641-7835]

Benefit for Norma Jean Croy, a Native American lesbian cultural political prisoner, with live music and lesbian / gay comedy
Sep 19 (sat) 7:00 pm at the Women's Building, 3543 18th Street (near Valencia) in SF [info (415) 285-1340] ($10 to $15 suggested)

Benefit for the Kuna Indians of Panama with Puksu Igualikinya, the International Kuna representative, speaking on the unique relationship between the Kuna and their homeland, rainforest, and islands; opening ceremony with Gina Pacaldo; singing; crafts
Sep 19 (sat) 8:00 pm at Gathering Tribes, 1309-F Solano (near Pomona) in Albany [Gathering Tribes (510) 525-1265] ($6)

Haiti: Killing the Dream film on the terror and repression now being endured by the Haitian people following the 1991 coup
Sep 21 & 22 (mon/tue) 7:15 & 9:15 pm at Roxie Cinema, 3117 16th St (at Valencia) in SF [Roxie (415) 863-1087] filmmakers present
Sep 23 (wed) 5:00, 7:00, & 9:00 pm at UC Theatre, University Av at Shattuck in Berkeley [UC Theatre (510) 843-6267]

Lesbian & Gay Community Meeting to Organize Participation in the Internatnl Tribunal & the Oct 11 Resistance 500 Demo
Sep 23 (wed) 7:30 pm at New College, 766 Valencia Street (near 19th) in SF [LAGAI (510) 654-8465 or (415) 558-8671]

Resistance 500 Posting Party to publicize the International Tribunal and Resistance 500 demonstrations [AIM (415) 552-1992]
Sep 26 (sat) 10:00 am meet at the American Indian Movement office, 2940 16th Street (one block east of Mission) in SF

A Cultural Evening in Commemoration of 500 Years of Resistance of Indigenous People, with Aztec dance, Native American dance & ceremony, Andean music, marimba concert, artistic presentation, & Guatemalan food, drinks, textiles, and books
Sep 26 (sat) 6:30 to 10:00 pm at Saint Peter's Church, 1249 Alabama (at 24th) in SF [info (415) 824-2534 or (415) 550-9225]

Incident at Oglala (Leonard Peltier video) shown at a benefit for the International Tribunal of Indigenous Peoples, plus a video on the 500 years of resistance activities in Guatemala, Bobby Castillo of American Indian Movement, and Native American drummers
Sep 26 (sat) 8:00 pm doors open at Klub Komotion, 2779 16th Street (near Folsom) in SF [AIM (415) 552-1992] ($5 to $7)

Our Insistence on 500(0) Years of Resistance multi-kulti performances exercising & exorcising the oppression, resistance, culture, & over-culture of the people of the place now called America; plus post-show discussion ($5 to $10)
Sep 26 (sat) and Sep 27 (sun) 8:30 pm at 848 Divisadero (at McAllister) in SF [info (415) 885-1602 or (415) 885-2003]

After Columbus Landed: A Native American Art Exhibit [SFSU Art Gallery (415) 338-2580] (free)
Sep 30 (wed) thru Oct 22 (thu) 10 to 6 mon-thu, 10 to 3 friday, at the SFSU Student Union Art Gallery, 19th & Holloway in SF

Spiritual Genocide Forum addressing the charge by Indigenous peoples of new age misuse of their symbols and traditions with Edna Seidner (Elder from the Bear River and Weott Tribes), Anita Poree (Creole / Chactow composer, poet, and essayist), Miguel Molina (IITC), and John Lavelle (Center for the SPIRIT) [Sonoma County Rainbow Greens (707) 545-8426]
Sep 30 (wed) 7:00 pm at the Copperfield Annex, 650 Fourth Street in Santa Rosa (free) [Copperfield Annex (707) 545-5326]

International Tribunal of Indigenous Peoples and Oppressed Nationalities in the USA led by the American Indian Movement
A unique global gathering of people of color to testify on and discuss the systematic violation of their human rights & international law
1992: 500 years of resistance to genocide, colonialism, and political internment beginning with Columbus' "discovery" on Oct 12
Thursday: community events; Friday 7:30 cultural event; Saturday 10 to 10: testimony; Sunday 10 to 3: panel and workshops
Oct 1 thru 4 (thu thru sun) at Mission High School, 18th Street & Dolores in SF [American Indian Movement (415) 552-1992]

Nevada Test Site Indigenous Forum and Ceremony "Healing Global Wounds"; Stop Nuclear Testing; End 500 Years of Injustice
Oct 2 to 4: Indigenous People's Forum in Las Vegas; Oct 5: Demonstration at the Test Site Operations Office in Las Vegas
Oct 5 to 9: Join European Peace Pilgrimage & Walk Across America for Mother Earth for the final 65-mile leg of their 3000-mile walk
Oct 6 to 12: Nevada Test Site Encampment; Oct 10: Native-led Healing Ceremony
Oct 11: Multicultural Rally and Mass Nonviolent Action; Oct 12: 500 Years Commemoration
[in Las Vegas: American Peace Test (702) 386-9834; Citizen Alert (702) 648-8962; Nevada Desert Experience (702) 646-4814]
Oct 2 thru 12 in Las Vegas and at the Nevada Test Site Nuclear Testing Alert Hotline (702) 386-9831

The Appearance of Civilization an anti-Columbus theatrical event on the beach at night with audience participation
Audience members will wear walkmans and march with masked conquistadors thru a surreal landscape of parallel histories
Oct 2 & 3 (fri & sat) 8:00 pm previews Oct 9, 10, 16, 17 (fri & sat) 8:00 pm full show at Rodeo Beach in the Marin Headlands
Oct 23, 24, 29, 30 (fri & sat) 8:00 pm at Ocean Beach in SF ($14.92; previews are half that) [Antenna Theater (415) 332-4862]

Beyond 1992: Dis-Covering American Culture symposium sponsored by the Mexican Museum [info (415) 441-0445]
Institutional racism in museums, artistic practice and ethnic & social identity, Spanish Conquest destruction of Mexican archives...
Oct 3 & 4 (sat & sun) 10:00 am to 4:00 pm at the Magic Theater, Fort Mason Building D, 3rd Floor, Laguna & Marina in SF

Third Annual Chesky of Auto-Descubrimiento a performance / procession to celebrate indigenous cultures of the Americas
Oct 4 (sun) 1:00 pm starting at Dolores Park, Dolores at 18th Street in SF [American Indian Movement (415) 552-1992]
Wise Fool Puppet Intervention will perform; to participate in mask-making, puppet-building, or performance call (415) 905-5958

Art In Chains: The Art of Leonard Peltier and Native American Prisoner Artists [American Indian Movement (415) 552-1992]
Oct 7 (wed) grand opening at the Mission Cultural Center, 2868 Mission Street (below 24th) in SF; show runs Sep 18 thru Oct 17

Watershed: A Dramatization of Oral Histories a new play dramatizing the Salmon War of 1978, a conflict between Yurok Indians and federal agents over the salmon of California's Klamath River; Talespinners Theater with the Turtle Island Ensemble ($10 & $12)
Oct 7 thru 10 (wed thru sat) at the Julia Morgan Theater, 2640 College (at Derby) in Berkeley [Mill Valley Arts Cmsn (415) 383-7818]

Four Directions: Women Honor Native Lands art opening by Taller Sin Fronteras, w/ Jean LaMarr, Sharol Graves, & Sara Bates
Oct 7 (wed) 7:00 pm (show runs through Nov 14) at Pro Arts, 461 Ninth Street (at Broadway) in Oakland [info (510) 763-4361] (free)

Benefit Dinner for Native American Political Prisoner Leonard Peltier [American Indian Movement (415) 552-1992]
Oct 9 (fri) at the Intertribal Friendship House, 523 East 14th Street (near 5th Avenue) in Oakland

Some Resistance 500 Events (continued)

Berkeley Indigenous Peoples Day with representatives from many of the Native Nations of Turtle Island (continental America)
Oct 10 (sat) 11:00 am to 2:00 pm in MLKing Park, Allston at MLKing in Berkeley; then 2:00 to 4:00 pm at Shattuck & Allston
Turtle Island Monument dedication, food, music, poetry, theater, crafts, & info [Berkeley Resistance 500 Task Force (510) 464-0346]

Truth in History: The First Nations InterTribal Gathering with native music, orators, arts & crafts booths, authentic Native
American food, large memorial participation painting, Indian face painting, finger painting, and exhibits [Info (510) 452-1235]
Oct 10 (sat) 12:00 noon to sundown at the Intertribal Friendship House & nearby Clinton Park, East 14th at 8th Av in Oakland

Motorcade and Parade from Berkeley to Oakland for the First Nations Intertribal Gathering [Info (510) 569-2834]
Oct 10 (sat) 3:00 pm from Berkeley Indigenous Peoples Day to the Intertribal Friendship House at 523 East 14th Street in Oakland

Resistance 500 Concerts at Shoreline Amphitheater in Mountain View [tickets available by mail from BASS: (510) 762-BASS]
Oct 10 (sat) 2:00 pm with Circle of Elders, Carlos Santana, Oren Lyons, and Thomas Banyaca ($25 reserved; $15 lawn from BASS)
Oct 11 (sun) 2:00 pm with Floyd "Red Crow" Westerman, The Cult, Don Henley, and others ($25 reserved; $19.50 lawn from BASS)

Demonstration Against the Re-enactment of the Columbus Landing [American Indian Movement (415) 552-1992]
Oct 11 (sun) 9:00 am civil disobedience & legal demo at Aquatic Park, Beach Street & Van Ness in SF; 12:00 march; 1:00 rally

Alcatraz Sunrise Ceremony on the International Day of Solidarity with Indigenous Peoples call IITC about ferry tickets
Oct 12 (mon) 5:00 am on Alcatraz Island in the San Francisco Bay [International Indian Treaty Council (415) 566-0251]

Mending the Circle: A Gathering for Worship and Nonviolent Witness in Solidarity with Indigenous People
Gather around the Columbus statue at Colt tower to tell the historical truth behind this innocent-looking statue
Oct 12 (mon) 10:00 am on Telegraph Hill Blvd, near Kearney & Lombard in SF [Ecumenical Peace Institute / CALC (510) 444-5701]

Press Conference and Teach-in on Truth in History regarding the mythological Columbus and our discovery of him on our shores
Oct 12 (mon) 10:00 am press conference; 12:00 noon teach-in, at UC Berkeley's Sproul Plaza, Telegraph & Bancroft in Berkeley

Concert at Crissy Field on the International Day of Solidarity with Indigenous Peoples
Oct 12 (mon) 12:00 noon at Crissy Field in the Presidio of SF (between Mason Street and Marine Drive) [IITC (415) 566-0251]

Fast for Freedom and Justice a relay fast to mobilize public support for political prisoners Leonard Peltier, geronimo ji Jaga
(Pratt), & Norma Jean Croy; beginning Oct 12 in SF with an individual 46-day fast (to Thanksgiving), the fast will then continue in
relay fashion throughout the country; distribution of educational materials and petitions are the main focus [Info (415) 541-5651]

Oct 13 (tue) — Day of Rest to "Unplug Mother Earth" the Bay Area Regional Indian Alliance asks that we do not participate in
dominant culture activities, such as driving, shopping, and television; "Do Not Buy Today" [Regional Indian Alliance (510) 452-1235]

Post-Columbus Debrief & Salon an attempt to learn from recent Quincentennial events, both "alternative" and state-financed
Oct 15 (thu) 7:30 pm at 848 Divisadero (at McAllister) in SF [Info (415) 885-1602, (415) 885-2003] (donations accepted)

A Circle of Indigenous People with the Turtle Island Ensemble Theater Arts, hosted by American Indian Contemporary Arts
Oct 16 (fri) 7:00 pm at the San Francisco Arts Institute, 800 Chestnut (at Jones) in SF [Info (415) 495-7600]

Public Hearings on Hate Crimes to educate on and call for action against the current proliferation of hate crimes
[Unified Against Genocide: 1992 (a new coalition formed in resistance to celebrations of Columbus' invasion) (415) 826-1054]
Oct 24 (sat) all day at the First Congregational Church, 2501 Harrison in Oakland (3 blocks north of Grand Avenue)

Picket the Film "Columbus: The Discovery", a multi-million dollar Big Lie from the creators of "Superman"
The filmmakers say "This is an upbeat adventure film; if you want to know what happened to the Indians, go make your own movie"
Fridays 6:45 pm at the Galaxy Theater, Van Ness & Sutter Street in SF [American Indian Movement (415) 552-1992]

Indian News Network Television Show c/o Alvin Meriweather, KMTP Channel 32, 1131 Sutter St., #200, SF CA 94109
Last monday of each month (including July 27) on KMTP Channel 32; call for times [Info (415) 567-6513]

Living on Indian Time Radio Show [contact Dennis Jennings, Cathy Chapman, Titus Frenchman, or Yvonne Swan at KPFA]
Fridays at 8:00 pm on KPFA Radio, 94.1 FM [KPFA (510) 848-6767]

World Beat Dance with DJ Doug Wendt, plus tabling by Resistance 500! ($3 to $4) partial proceeds benefit Resistance 500!
Every Sunday 9:00 pm to 2:00 am at the Kennel Club, 628 Divisadero Street (between Hayes & Grove) in SF

For more information contact the Resistance 500 Coalition at (510) 452-1235 523 East 14th Street, Oakland 94606
a coalition of community activists and representatives of organizations committed to organizing alternative activities during 1992
To add events to this calendar, contact Ken Cheetham at (510) 848-9582 ext. 3 (fax is ext. 4) POBox 11232, Berkeley 94701-2232
Call Life on the Water Theatre's Quincentenary Hotline for additional event information at (415) 885-4749 fax: (415) 885-4257
Please reprint this calendar and directory and redistribute them in your community!

56

IITC Conference and Concerts

IITC held the 14th International Indian Treaty Conference October 5-9 at San Francisco State University, with a focus on the struggles of California Indians and plans for the 1993 International Year of the World's Indigenous Peoples. Special guest from the UN was Dr. Miguel Alfonso Martinez.

The Treaty Council also sponsored three days of Resistance 500 concerts.

Artists at the Treaty Council Concerts

Two concerts were held at Shoreline Ampitheater in Mountain View.

On October 10 was All Our Colors: the Good Road Concert, with Circle of Elders, Carlos Santana, Oren Lyons, Thomas Banyaca John Trudell, The Wagon Burners, Jackson Browne, Mickey Hart. John Lee Hooker, Red Thunder, and others.

On October 11 was Healing the Sacred Hoop: The Next 500 Years, with Floyd "Red Crow" Westerman, Bonnie Raitt, Buffy Sainte-Marie, The Cult, Don Henley, and others.

On October 12, they offered a free concert at Crissy Field in San Francisco's Golden Gate Park, with many of the same performers.

•

ALL OUR COLORS
THE GOOD ROAD CONCERT

SANTANA
JACKSON BROWNE
MICKEY HART
AND FRIENDS
JOHN LEE HOOKER
JOHN TRUDELL
WHITE BOY
AND THE WAGON BURNERS
RED THUNDER

SATURDAY
OCTOBER 10 • 2PM
A benefit for the Traditional Circle
of Elders and Youth

Shoreline
AMPHITHEATRE • AT • MOUNTAIN • VIEW

SUNDAY, OCT 11

HEALING THE SACRED HOOP
THE NEXT 500 YEARS

BONNIE RAITT

Special Acoustic Performances By
DON HENLEY
PAHINUI BROTHERS
WITH RY COODER
& DAVID LINDLEY
TODD RUNDGREN
BUFFY SAINTE-MARIE
FLOYD "RED CROW" WESTERMAN

SUNDAY
OCTOBER 11 • 2PM
A benefit for the International
Indian Treaty Council

Shoreline
AMPHITHEATRE • AT • MOUNTAIN • VIEW

MUSIC AND CULTURAL GATHERING
HEALING THE SACRED HOOP:
THE NEXT 500 YEARS
MONDAY, OCT 12

A day of music and inspiration. The gathering will
take place at **Crissy Field**, in **San Francisco**, on
Monday, October 12, at **11AM**. Admission is free.

AIM Tribunal

Between October 9-11, the American Indian Movement (AIM) organized a three-day International Tribunal of Indigenous People and Oppressed Nationalities in the USA.

INTERNATIONAL
TRIBUNAL
OF INDIGENOUS PEOPLES
AND OPPRESSED NATIONS
IN THE USA

OCTOBER 1-4, 1992

SAN FRANCISCO, CA

1992

500 YEARS OF RESISTANCE TO
GENOCIDE, COLONIALISM AND
POLITICAL INTERNMENT

AIM Demonstration Against the Re-enactment
Peace Navy Stops Columbus

San Francisco's large Italian-American population traditionally thought of October 12 as a celebration of Italian-American culture and heritage (not as a celebration of imperialism), and many were dismayed by the situation. Undaunted by the cancellation of the arrival of the Columbus ship replicas (see page 71), the San Francisco Columbus Day Committee soldiered on with plans for their annual Columbus Day Parade and Re-enactment of the Columbus Landing at Aquatic Park, in which an actor dressed in a Columbus costume arrives in a small boat, falls on one knee and claims San Francisco for the King and Queen of Spain.

On October 11, 1992, AIM held an important Demonstration Against the Re-enactment of the Columbus Landing at Aquatic Park in San Francisco, followed by a march. During the demonstration the Peace Navy, with over 150 boats, strung ropes between their vessels, and prevented Columbus's boat from landing. After that, we marched in a counter-parade.

Eventually clearer heads prevailed, and in 1994 the parade organizers changed the name (and focus) to the Italian Heritage Parade.

•

University of California Teach-In

On October 12 a teach-in and press conference on the theme "Truth In History regarding the mythological Christopher Columbus and our discovery of him on our shores" was held on Sproul Plaza at the University of California, Berkeley, cosponsored by the Bay Area Regional Indian Alliance.

A group of actors recreates its version of the landing of Columbus at UC-Berkeley's Sproul Plaza. Marc Kolsters, right, 'kills' two Native Americans.

[*Oakland Tribune* 10/13/1992]

•

UnPlug North America

On October 13 the Bay Area Regional Indian Alliance and the Indigenous Environmental Network sponsored a Day of Rest to Unplug North America to Give Mother Earth A Rest. They asked that we "not participate in dominant culture activities," to use only sustainable energy, and to not conduct any business transactions.

Peace and Dignity Journeys

Peace and Dignity Journeys' first run in 1992 was "a prayer to heal our nations" and the world. The plan was that runners would begin in April 1992 from Alaska running south and from Argentina running north. The runners would pass through numerous Indigenous communities, where they would share wisdom and collect ceremonial objects symbolically containing the prayers of all the many Native peoples, and all would come together for final ceremonies at the base of the Pyramid of the Sun in Teotihuacán, Mexico on October 12, 1992. Their inspiration came from two sources: the Andean prophesy of the condor and eagle, and the prophesies of spiritual running passed down from elders in many parts of Indigenous America. Those running prophesies foretold that spiritual running would help the Native nations to reunite: "We are like a body that was broken up into pieces and this body will come back together to be whole again." Dorinda Moreno, of Hi-Tec Aztec Productions, was a key California organizer. The success of the first Peace & Dignity Journey of 1992 began the tradition of a run every four years thereafter.

63

Museum Dedication

Besides operating museums in the City, the University of California at Berkeley also operated the Black Hawk Museum of Art, Science & Culture in the town of that name, around 25 miles inland. A member of our group, Marilyn Jackson, pointed this out to Dennis Jennings, who was a descendent of Black Hawk, the great Sac and Fox chief. That led to Dennis and our group helping to organize a weekend of Indigenous events at that location the following spring, when the Blackhawk Museum was dedicated to the Sac and Fox Nation.

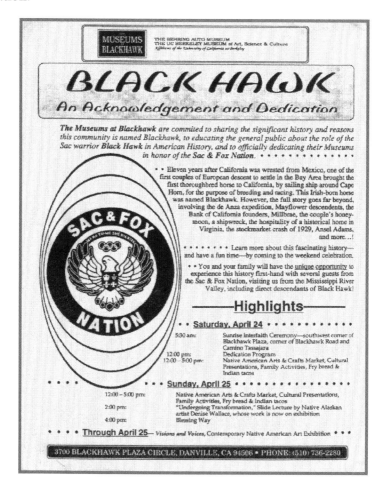

Berkeley-Yurok Sister Communities

Another important project of ours was helping to organize a Berkeley-Yurok Nation "sister community" relationship. For that we worked closely with Sue Masten, who was later elected tribal chair and then president of the National Congress of American Indians (NCIA). A group of us traveled to the Yurok Reservation in northwestern California on the Klamath River near the Pacific coast, and were guests of their generous hospitality. The Berkeley City Council approved the Yuroks as a sister community the following year.

Sue Masten and Mark Gorrell

The Chasky

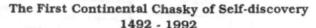

1990 Chasky Poster

On Saturday, October 3, 1992, the week before the quincentenary, the third annual Chasky was held in San Francisco's Mission District. The original *chaskys* 500 years previously were relay runners who delivered messages over long distances across the Andes during Inca times. The modern Chasky used the relay concept to carry messages to the people today.

The 1992 San Francisco Chasky began in Dolores Park, and finished in La Raza Park with rituals, music, poetry, dance, and speakers at different street corners. The performance installations en route were coordinated by Luis Vasquez, and included Wise Fool Puppet Intervention, Teatro ng Tanan, Pearl Ubungen Dancers, Earth Circus, Francisco X. Alarcon, Roots Against War, Grupo Maya Kusamej Junan, and others.

The Chasky began two years previously, in 1990.

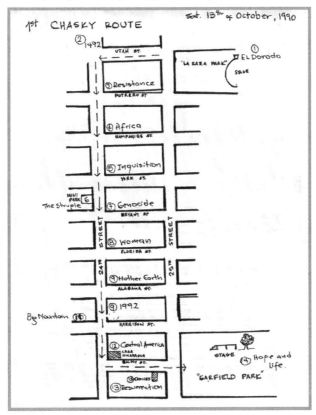

The Committee of Five Hundred Years of Self-Discovery, a coalition of about 25 progressive political and cultural groups, was the organizing force behind the Chasky. Members included the South and Meso-American Indian Information Center, the Treaty Council, the American Indian Movement, and the Alliance for Cultural

67

Democracy. Members of our Berkeley committee were involved. The 1990 Chasky was the first major counter-quincentennial event in the Bay Area, held three months after the Quito Encuentro. Among the core members of the organizing group were Samuel Guía, Rodrigo Betancur, Juanita Rieloff, Felipe Acosta, and Luis Vasquez.

We scheduled the first Chasky for Saturday, October 13, 1990. The first Chasky flyer stated that it was "An invitation to recover our historic memory... to rescue our own identity and self-determination of the People... Inspired by the spirit of defense of Mother Earth and the Resistance of the native people of the Americas and African American people. We have joined with solidarity organizations and artists to respond to the Jubilee celebrations of so-called 'Discovery of The Americas', when in fact there was no such discovery, and in reality we have had five centuries of oppression and Resistance, to a system foreign to life."

Poster by Rodrigo Betancur and Elizabeth Dante

The Chasky procession started at the stage in La Raza Park on 25th Street, San Francisco, with ceremonies, speakers, and music. The crowd then walked to 24th street and turned east, gathering passersby as we proceeded. At each corner for ten blocks was a cultural presentation on a different theme: 1492; Resistance; Africa; Inquisition; The Struggle; Genocide; Women; Mother Earth; 1992;

68

Big Mountain; Central America; Resurrection. It finished with another round of ceremonies, speakers, and music on the Garfield Park stage, where the theme was Hope and Life. The Chasky was a very successful event.

Azteca Dancers lead "Chasky" procession/performance piece through the heart of San Francisco's Mission

[*Huracán* Fall/Winter 1990]

First Chasky

The following year, on October 12, 1991, with Luis Vasquez as the central organizer, the Chasky reversed the route, beginning in Garfield Park and finishing in La Raza Park. It again used "a variety of performances and visual art as a strong statement of cultural, spiritual, and political identity," and meant to be "a rallying point and touchstone for many groups... to work in harmony to dedicate the next twelve months to opposing the quincentenary celebrations in 1992."

The first two San Francisco Chaskys did not actually declare October 12 to be Indigenous Peoples Day, although the Chaskys included the same themes.

For the first Berkeley Indigenous Peoples Day in October, 1992, we adopted the *chasky* concept in our Procession and Indigenous Peoples Parade on Shattuck Avenue.

After the fourth Chasky in 1993, the organizing group disbanded, with the evaluation that the Chasky had not become a self-sustaining tradition, perhaps partly because it had become more focused on opposition than on positive energies working to shape the future. However, the concept was revived and another San Francisco Chasky was held in the year 2000.

•

The Quincentenary Debacle

As discussed earlier (see page 8), the spark that touched off Indigenous Peoples Day in Berkeley was the Bay Area being designated by the US Congress as the center of a planned gala national celebration of the 500th anniversary of Columbus's landfall. In the Bay Area, the US Columbus Commission set up a local committee under the joint honorary chair of the mayors of San Francisco, Oakland, and San Jose, and told them they needed to raise $1.5 million.

Spain built the ships, but Texaco pulled out of its $5 million commitment, leaving the Columbus Commission holding the bag. By 1990 the Bay Area committee was in a $700,000 hole, with the first director resigning under charges of financial misconduct. Still they conjured up a new chair and soldiered on. In June, 1990, San Francisco Mayor Art Agnos and George F Jewett, Jr., Chairman of the San Francisco Bay Christopher Columbus Quincentenary Jubilee Committee, tried to drum up enthusiasm and support, and sent the following letter to mayors of most of the other Bay Area cities. Perhaps sensing trouble, they omitted Berkeley Mayor Loni Hancock from the list.

•

Office of the Mayor
SAN FRANCISCO

ART AGNOS

June 1, 1990

The Honorable Marie Daniels
Mayor
City of San Pablo
City Hall
One Alvarado Square
San Pablo, CA 94806

Dear Mayor Daniels,

As you know, 1992 will mark the 500th anniversary of Christopher Columbus's first voyage to the New World. International celebrations are already in the works and the Christopher Columbus Quincentenary Jubilee Commission in Washington D.C. has selected San Francisco as the site for America's celebration on Columbus Day, October 12th of that year. The eyes of the nation will be upon us as media and spectators converge on the Bay Area to participate in and witness an international parade of Tall Ships, replicas of the Niña, Pinta, and Santa Maria, fireworks, parades and a uniquely exciting historic celebration. The Bay Area will be the center of not only national but worldwide interest as the Columbus Quincentenary is being observed throughout Europe and Latin America as well.

The San Francisco Bay Christopher Columbus Quincentenary Jubilee Committee will be organizing the grand celebration itself as well as other festivities that will take place throughout the Bay Area. We are currently working on many plans and projects that are possibilities for this celebration. A key to this event is that we showcase and include the entire region, not just a single city. This celebration will present us with an unparalleled opportunity to demonstrate to the world the tremendous diversity and beauty of our region, and it is our hope that all of the San Francisco Bay Area will be involved.

We are writing you today to briefly inform you of these plans and to assure you that we will be contacting you and your colleagues in the near future in order to solicit your input and involvement in the planning of this celebration. We look forward to the regional festivities in October of 1992 and to your participation in this historic event.

Most sincerely,

Art Agnos
Mayor

George F. Jewett, Jr.
Chairman
The San Francisco Bay
 Christopher Columbus
 Quincentenary Jubilee Committee

72

Fate of the Columbus Quincentenary

On August 10, 1992, soon after the replicas of Columbus's ships arrived in Boston Harbor, the co-chair of the Columbus Quincentenary was sad to announce that the ships would not continue their voyage to the west coast. "The technical and logistical obstacles would daunt even a Don Quixote," she said.

The San Francisco Bay Columbus Committee, and all the other west coast cities, had been unable to raise any funds, much less $1.5 million, in part because Resistance 500 and all our associated groups had done our job.

So two months before the quincentenary, they folded. The whole elaborate shebang was cancelled. We had won.

In an article about it, the *Oakland Tribune* wrote,

> The cancellation was called a minor victory by opponents of the traditional Columbus Day holiday who would rather celebrate the lives of the indigenous people — whose fates were forever changed by Columbus's landing. Lee Sprague, a Native American artist, saw the ships on their visit to New York, and hated the thought of them coming to the Bay Area. "The Columbus ships were the forerunners of these huge military aircraft carriers. They were both the instruments of suppression and occupation."[6]

The people of the Bay Area didn't want to celebrate what the ships stood for. Instead, we wanted to celebrate Indigenous Peoples Day.

•

CHAPTER TWO

The 1977 Geneva UN Conference
The first declaration of Indigenous Peoples Day

Fifteen years before 1992, a conference in Geneva, Switzerland, played a crucial role in this history: the 1977 UN Conference in which Native Nations first called for Indigenous Peoples Day.

"One of the most important things to come out of the Geneva Conference did not get much attention at the time, even though it was the first item of the program of action in the final resolutions. It reads: ... **"to observe October 12, the day of so-called 'discovery' of America, as an international day of solidarity with the indigenous peoples of the Americas."** Why is that so important? ... It means that we have made a very large part of the world recognize who we are and even to stand with us in solidarity in our long fight. From now on, children all over the world will learn the true story of American Indians on Columbus Day instead of a pack of lies about three European ships."[7]

Jimmie Durham, 1977

The delegation arrives at the Geneva conference.
First Declaration of Indigenous Peoples Day
at the 1977 Geneva UN Conference

One day early in 1992, Millie Ketcheshawno brought a book into an Indigenous Peoples Day Committee meeting, *Basic Call to Consciousness*. Millie, one of the founders of Berkeley Indigenous Peoples Day, had been an early activist on the Alcatraz occupation back in 1969 and the first woman director of Inter-Tribal Friendship House in Oakland. She said that we all needed to read the book, and her copy circulated around the committee. [8]

The book was mostly about the 1977 Geneva conference which first proclaimed Indigenous Peoples Day, including a first-hand account of the conference by José Barreiro. The book also contained the message of the Haudenosaunee (Iroquois) nation to the world, as drafted by John Mohawk and approved by their Grand Council of Chiefs, explaining that the Haudenosaunee had come to Geneva to speak for the natural world, for the future generations, and for life on this planet, which were all were at great risk, and therefore we each needed to contribute to the solution.

Basic Call to Consciousness greatly deepened our committee's understanding of the profound issues at hand.

BASIC CALL to CONSCIOUSNESS

Preamble ◆ Chief Oren Lyons
Introduction ◆ John Mohawk
Afterword ◆ José Barreiro

edited by Akwesasne Notes

Phillip Deere, Grandfather David Monongye, and Hoyaneh Tadadaho
(Leon Schenadoah), heading the procession to the Opening Plenary
Session.

The International NGO Conference on Discrimination Against
Indigenous Populations in the Americas, held at the United Nations'
offices in Geneva on September 20-23, 1977, was a watershed event,
the very first UN conference with Indigenous delegates, the first
direct entry of Native peoples into international affairs, the first time
that Native peoples were able to speak for themselves at the UN.
Some governments felt so threatened that they prevented delegates
from participating and persecuted them upon return.

Following a Lakota pipe ceremony and opening presentations,
Russell Means made the keynote speech, followed by more than a

hundred Native representatives detailing systematic abuses of their human rights and the expropriation and destruction of their lands and natural resources by governments and corporations.

The Geneva event was the product of many hands and minds. One key person who brought it about, but did not actually attend, was Jimmie Durham, Cherokee artist-poet, first director of the International Indian Treaty Council (IITC). According to Roxanne Dunbar-Ortiz, who was an IITC staff member at the conference, Durham played a pivotal role.[9]

Durham lived in Geneva, Switzerland in the late 1960s and early 1970s, where he became involved with the progressive international community. There he came up with the concept of the conference, and convinced several important non-governmental organizations (NGOs) to sponsor the idea.

According to Dunbar-Ortiz's account, from his home in Switzerland, Durham followed the rebirth of Native activism in the United States, starting with the 1969 occupation of Alcatraz, the 1972 American Indian Movement (AIM) seizure of the Bureau of Indian Affairs building in Washington DC, and the over two month siege at Wounded Knee on the Pine Ridge Sioux reservation. Durham returned to the United States, met with AIM leaders, and proposed the project that was realized in the June 1974 founding of the International Indian Treaty Council, (IITC) which Durham headed for the following six years. In 1977, the IITC gained non-governmental organization status in the United Nations Economic and Social Council (ECOSOC), the primary body in which NGOs interfaced on the UN international stage.

The IITC initiated the Geneva conference and invited most of the Indigenous organizations and delegates. The event was logistically organized through a grouping of international organizations called the Special NGO Committee on Human Rights.

Over 250 people participated in the Geneva conference. Delegates represented over sixty indigenous peoples and Native nations, from fifteen American countries: Argentina, Bolivia, Canada, Chile, Costa Rica, Guatemala, Ecuador, Mexico, Nicaragua, Panama, Paraguay, Peru, Suriname, the United States, and Venezuela. Over fifty international NGOs, UN agencies, and 27 UN member states also sent representatives and observers.

The world press attended, including José Barreiro (Ismaelillo), coeditor of *Akwesakne Notes*, who wrote a firsthand account of the proceedings in *Basic Call to Consciousness*.[10]

While most of the delegates were aligned with IITC and AIM, the organizing committee also invited other Indigenous groups affiliated with WCIP, the World Council of Indigenous Peoples. WCIP had disagreements with IITC and AIM in perspectives and alliances. WCIP and some of its affiliates received organizational funding from the Canadian and US governments, while AIM and IITC had a somewhat adversarial relationship with governments. Organizational frictions were present before and during the conference, but did not undercut the work in the end.

The conference produced the first draft of what eventually became the UN Declaration on the Rights of Indigenous Peoples, and resolved:

> The representatives of the indigenous peoples gave evidence to the international community of the ways in which discrimination, genocide and ethnocide operated. While the situation may vary from country to country, the roots are common to all: they include the brutal colonization to open the way for the plunder of their land and resources by commercial interests seeking maximum profits; the massacres of millions of native peoples for centuries and the continuous grabbing of their land which deprives them of the possibility of developing their own resources and means of livelihood; the denial of self-determination of indigenous nations and peoples destroying their traditional value system and their social and cultural fabric. The evidence pointed to the combination of this oppression resulting in the further destruction of the indigenous nations...

PROGRAMME OF ACTIONS

The Conference recommends:

• **to observe October 12, the day of so-called "discovery" of America, as an International Day of Solidarity with the Indigenous Peoples of the Americas**

So the very first item of the "Programme of Actions" was to celebrate October 12th as Indigenous Peoples Day. The full text of the Final Resolution and the complete Programme of Actions, is in Appendix F, on page 198. The draft declaration that 30 years later became the basis of the UN Declaration on the Rights of Indigenous Peoples is in Appendix G, page 203.

The 1977 Geneva conference had far-reaching repercussions, including the establishment several years later of the permanent UN Working Group on Indigenous Populations (WGIP), with the mandate "to review developments pertaining to the promotion and protection of human rights and fundamental freedoms of indigenous peoples; to give attention to the evolution of international standards concerning indigenous rights."[11]

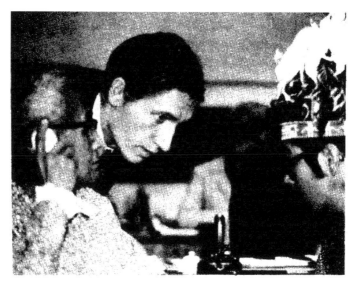

The International Indian Treaty Council reported back from the conference in its publication *Treaty Council News*. The report back issue included speeches by many of the delegates and the texts of the Conference resolutions. The conference photos in these pages are from this document, which is published on the United Nations web site (photographer not credited in original).[12]

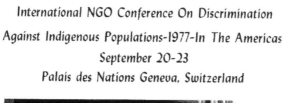

International NGO Conference On Discrimination
Against Indigenous Populations-1977-In The Americas
September 20-23
Palais des Nations Geneva, Switzerland

THE GENEVA CONFERENCE

Official Report by: INTERNATIONAL INDIAN TREATY COUNCIL
777 United Nations Plaza, New York, N.Y.10017

SPECIAL ISSUE: TREATY COUNCIL NEWS OCTOBER 1977 VOL. 1 NO. 7
American Indian Treaty Council Information Center
870 Market Street San Francisco, CA. 94102

In the following years, other struggles and priorities occupied the Treaty Council, but Indigenous Peoples Day rose again as a priority as the 500th anniversary of 1492 approached.

Among the Participants in Geneva

Native nations from the USA sent a thirteen member delegation, plus staff and observers. In addition, the Iroquois (Haudenosaunee) Federation sent a separate delegation of twelve, plus several observers. Four of the US delegates were affiliated with IITC: Russell Means (Lakota), David Monongye (Hopi, Hotevilla), Phillip Deere (Muscogee), Larry Red Shirt (Lakota).

AIM delegates were Pat Bellanger (Ojibwa) and Clyde Bellecourt (Anishinabe-Ojibwe). An additional fifteen Native people from the USA came as staff and observers, seven of whom were affiliated with the IITC, including Peggy Phelps Means (Lakota), Bill Means (Lakota), Winona Leduke (Ojibwa), and Roxanne Dunbar-Ortiz. Others included Marie-Helene Laraque (Taino), Joe Lafferty (Sioux), Marie Sanchez (Northern Cheyenne), and David Spotted Horse (Hunkpapa). The Iroquois delegation included Leon Shenadoah, Oren Lyons, and Audrey Shenandoah (Onondaga). Four of the seven Canadian delegates were affiliated with AIM Canada, including Ed Burnstick (Cree) and Art Solomon (Ojibwe). Ed Burnstick and Marie-Helene Laraque would also be at the 1990 Quito conference.

Indigenous delegates from Latin America included Jose Mendoza Acosta (Panama), Reinir Artist (Surinam, KANO), Antonio Millape (Mapuche, Chile), Rene Fuerst (Amazonia), Manuel Tzoc Mejia (Guatemala), Natalio Hernandez Hernandez (Mexico), Juan Condori Uriche (Bolivia), and Nilo Cayuqueo (Mapuche, Argentina). Cayuqueo would go on to become a key organizer of the Quito Encuentro of 1990, out of his office in Oakland, California.

CHAPTER THREE

The Condor and Eagle Gathering

Quito, Ecuador, 1990

A second watershed event in the history of Indigenous Peoples Day was the Quito Encuentro of 1990—the First Continental Gathering of Indigenous Peoples. For the first time, Indigenous peoples from the farthest north to the farthest south gathered together independently, without any government or official international body, and planned their resurgence and their future. The Encuentro had a great influence on the movement for justice for the Native nations of Turtle Island (Abya Yala, or the Americas).

At least three people who attended the 1977 Geneva conference were also in Quito: Nilo Cayuqueo, Ed Burnstick, and Marie-Helene Laraque.

Upon returning to their home countries from the Geneva conference in 1977, a number of the Latin American delegates had faced serious consequences for testifying. Cayuqueo, a Mapuche delegate from Argentina, had been a key organizer for Consejo Indio de SudAmerica, connected with the World Council of Indigenous Peoples (WCIP), the international group that was somewhat a rival at that time to the International Indian Treaty Council. Upon his return from Geneva, Cayuqueo found the military looking for him, but managed to get out of the country again, make it to Peru, and eventually to Oakland, California, where he founded the South and Meso-American Indian Information Center (SAIIC). Cayuqueo and SAIIC were instrumental in organizing the Encuentro of 1990. In this case, the Encuentro was an independent international indigenous conference, with neither the United Nations nor any nation-state directly involved. The North American contingent was officially led by Mexico. US and Canadian Indigenous Peoples were invited to the Gathering as individuals, but were not part of the organizing group, perhaps due to a problematic history between north and south. Different historical experiences resulted in divisions between Native peoples from Anglo and Hispanic colonized regions. That north-south divide contributed several years later to the World Council of Indigenous Peoples dissolving as an organization, while the International Indian Treaty Council continued to grow.

The Encuentro, the "gathering," the First Continental Conference of 500 Years of Indian Resistance (Primer Encuentro Continental de Pueblos Indios, 500 Años de Resistencia India), took place July 17-21, 1990. Indigenous Representatives from the Arctic Circle to the tip of South America were in attendance. A multinational Native meeting of this scope and magnitude had never before been attempted; it was a watershed for the indigenous peoples of the Americas. The Encuentro drew around 400 participants, with representatives from 120 different Indigenous nations, tribes, and organizations, as well as many nonIndian NGOs (non-governmental organizations).

Poster by Lligalo Abel

The Encuentro was called to examine the results of five centuries of colonial occupation, to coordinate activities around the upcoming 500th anniversary, and to plan political strategies for the future of Abya Yala (as they call this continent in the Andes, meaning "land in its full maturity" in the Panamanian Kuna language). Many governments of the world, including the USA, were sponsoring costly year-long 1992 "quincentennial" celebrations, and the Encuentro was intended to counter this from the Indigenous peoples' point of view that Columbus's voyage was not a "discovery," but the vanguard of an invasion.[13]

In the spring of 1990, after a discussion with Nilo Cayuqueo, Berkeley Mayor Loni Hancock appointed John Curl as her representative to the Encuentro, with the mission of seeking advice from the Native people of the hemisphere about how the city should respond to the coming Quincentenary

South and Meso-American Indian Information Center (SAIIC)

Mailing Address: P.O. Box 7550, Berkeley, CA 94707 USA
Office: 593 E. 14th St., Oakland, CA (415) 834-4963
Telex #: 154205417 SAIIC

May 16, 1990

Mayor Loni Hancock
City of Berkeley

Dear Mayor Hancock:

On behalf of our organization, I would like to invite you to attend and participate in an important conference to be held in Quito, Ecuador, July 17-21, 1990.

The conference, the "First Continental Conference of Indigenous Peoples on the 500 Years of Indian Resistance," will serve to coordinate counter-commemorations throughout the Americas, taking place in October, 1992, the quincentennial of Columbus' landing and the beginning of European imperialism in this hemisphere.

The broad objectives of this historical conference are:
1) to promote unity and active participation of Indigenous peoples and organizations in the 500 Years Campaign; 2) to promote a broad united front of participation by other sectors of society, including groups committed to human rights and protection of the natural world; 3) to reestablish intercultural exchanges between Indigenous peoples.

We know the City of Berkeley has a long record of public support for the struggles for social justice, and we hope Berkeley will work with us in creating a local counter-commemoration group. Some other cities, in contrast, are supporting official "celebrations", which are an insult to Indigenous people.

This conference will receive much international attention in the world press, and will launch counter-commemoration organizing groups throught the hemisphere. We want Berkeley to help play an important role in this project.

If you are unable to personally attend, please consider sending a delegate or a delegation in your place. We are already working closely on this project with John Curl, who will also be attending the conference. I would be glad to meet with you personally concerning this at your convenience.

Sincerely,

Nilo Cayuqueo
Director, SAIIC

Enclosed please find the conference agenda.

 **City of Berkeley**

July 3, 1990

Dear friends at the "First Continental Meeting of Indigenous Peoples--500 Years of Indian Resistance" Conference:

I regret not being able to attend in person, but offer all of you my warm greetings and solidarity from the City of Berkeley. I wish to use my offices to work with you because I believe we share many of the same goals.

For numerous generations, North American children have been taught the myth of a visionary European explorer, Christopher Columbus, who stumbled on a New World. There he was welcomed, the story goes, by the primitive inhabitants who were in awe of the superior cultural gifts of Europe Columbus brought. The childhood story ends with his return to Europe bringing the amazing news.

But of course the reality was far different. Historians tell us that Columbus returned to the New World with a great armada and proceeded to conquer and plunder wherever he went. His own writings clearly show this had always been his plan. Columbus, the original American Conquistador, presided over the destruction and enslavement of the Taino people of the Caribbean.

Yet generation after generation of North Americans, immigrants and their descendants, have clung to the myth and illusion, perhaps because the reality is so shockingly brutal.

We are now approaching the 500th anniversary of that fateful voyage. Governments of many nations, including the United States, are funding "Jubilee" commemorations, declaring a time of celebration. This midirected effort is based on the idea that colonization of the Americas represented a new beginning for oppressed people in a place where freedom was possible. Omitted is the price paid by indigenous people of the hemisphere, a price of oppression and genocide. This price was also paid by other peoples brought to this continent as slaves or as cheap labor; and the land itself has paid through exploitation and thoughtless environmental destruction.

Therefore, as Mayor of the City of Berkeley, California, I will call on all City agencies and the Berkeley school system to involve themselves in activities during the years 1991-1992 to educate our citizens about the historical facts of the colonization of this hemisphere and it effects on indigenous people. Our goal is to shape the future to rectify the historic injustices and create a society and natural environment that is free of oppression and exploitation.

Sincerely,

Loni Hancock, Mayor

89

The Encuentro booklet entitled Boletín *Informativo del Encuentro Continental del Pueblo Indígena* contained the conference schedule, most of which would actually take place not in the city of Quito, but up in the Andes mountains. It also contained the list of Indigenous and other organizations invited from various countries, registration and logistical information, an introduction, and statements about the Indigenous Uprising and the Condor and Eagle Prophesy.

Boletín Informativo
del
Encuentro Continental
del Pueblo Indígena

julio 17 - 21 - 1990
QUITO
ECUADOR

Because the complete original texts of these documents offer understanding in the words of the Encuentro organizers, here they are (in translation):

EDITORIAL of the ENCUENTRO

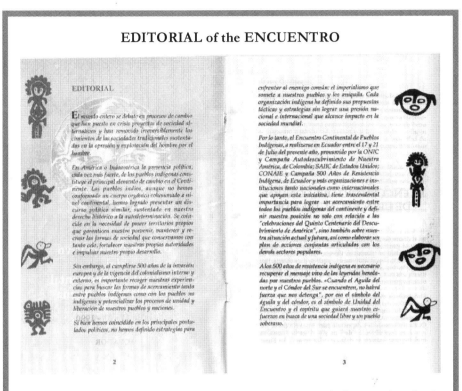

The entire world is debating the processes of change that have put into crisis alternative social projects and have irreversibly removed the bonding elements of traditional societies. These situations are maintained by the oppression and exploitation of humans by other humans.

In America, or Indoamerica, the ever increasing political presence of the indigenous peoples constitutes the principal element of change on the continent. Even though we Indian people have not formed a continental organizational body, we have arrived at a similar political point of view supported by our historical right to self determination. This coincides with the necessity to own our own territories to guarantee our future, to maintain and recreate the societal forms that we conserve so zealously, to fortify our own leadership and to take charge of our own development.

Nevertheless, after 500 years of European invasion and internal and external colonialism, it is important to confront our experiences to search for ways to bring together indigenous as well as non-indigenous peoples and to facilitate processes of unity as well as the liberation of our people and nations.

While we have concurred in the principal political positions, we have not defined strategies to confront our common enemy: the imperialism that oppresses and annihilates our peoples. Each indigenous organization has defined its own tactics and strategies without achieving a national and international pressure powerful enough to create an important impact on the world's societies at large.

For this reason, the Continental Encounter of Indigenous Peoples, taking place in Quito, Ecuador, July 17-21, 1990, promoted by ONIC and the Self Discovery of our America Campaign of Colombia; SAIIC of the United States; CONAIE and the 500 Years of Indigenous Resistance Campaign of Ecuador and other national and international organizations and institutions, takes on a transcendental importance, that of achieving a meeting of all the indigenous peoples of our continent, defining our position, not only with respect to the "celebrations of 500 years of the Discovery of America," but also with respect to our present and future situation, and elaborating a plan of action articulated jointly with other popular sectors.

After 500 years of indigenous Resistance, we must recuperate the living message of the legends inherited by our peoples. "When the Eagle of the North and the Condor of the South come together, there will be no force that can hold us back." This symbol of the eagle and the condor is the symbol of the Unity of the Encuentro and the spirit that guides our forces in the search of a free society and a sovereign people.

Su fuerza motivó a que el norte y el sur se unan, la unión de la gente del Norte con el Sur significaba también la unión del Cóndor y del Aguila. El Cóndor y el Aguila se tuvieron juntando sus lágrimas desde Jahanpacha (cielo) y Ucupacha (subsuelo). De esta unión brotó centro américa, en este trozo de tierra se concentró la sabiduría de Hanan y de Urin y se desarrollaron nuevas naciones, cuyos pobladores tuvieron la capacidad de sembrar la tierra en medio del gran océano y convertirlo a esto en lo que hoy es centro-américa.

Estos pueblos orientados por las leyes de Allpa Mama y Pacha Mama, tuvieron que atravesar situaciones difíciles, una de ellas fue la descuartización de sus naciones. Al producirse esta tragedia, los Willak Urmus instruyeron a sus Amautas, Curacas, Arawikus... etc, a crear profecías que orienten y guíen a nuestros pueblos. Estas profecías debían enseñar a las naciones indias a mantenerse sólidas, unidas y sobre todo, a buscar los caminos más adecuados para su liberación.

La iniciación de la liberación de los pueblos indios se simbolizaría con diferentes profecías, una de ellas, es la unión de las lágrimas de Cóndor de Urin y del Aguila de Hanan. La unión de estas de estas lágrimas soldarán nuestras heridas, fortalecerán el espíritu, el cuerpo y el pensamiento. El gran espíritu abrirá surco. En cada surco regará su semilla, y en cada paso brotarán batallones de hombres que expondrán sus pechos para rechazar las dagas del enemigo; extenderán sus manos para borrar la opresión, la explotación y la injusticia y escribirán en la gran hoja del cielo la sagrada palabra de Libertad.

La unión del Cóndor y del Aguila según la profecía debe producirse en este quinto siglo. El quinto siglo nacerá con nuevo espíritu. Este espíritu nuevo unirá nuevamente a las naciones indias del norte, centro y sud-américa.

5

EL ENCUENTRO DEL CONDOR DE URIN Y EL AGUILA DE HANAN

En el desarrollo de la vida de las Naciones Indias, cada cinco siglos se producen transformaciones de fondo y de forma. Estos cambios no pierden su esencia, van recubriéndose de nueva piel, la vieja se rejuvenece, se nutre de pura energía. Esta energía es transmitida por los grandes espíritus de la Allpa Mama y la Pacha Mama; es decir, de la naturaleza y del Universo en general.

Hace miles de años, cuando la vida inició su ciclo vital, Pachakamak (Dios del tiempo) creó a Inti (sol) y a Quilla (luna), de la unión de sus lágrimas y procreó a los Runas, a los hombres de este continente Appia –Yala (América). De la unión de Inti y de Quilla se desbordó la vida, en este parto brotó el Cóndor y el aguila; es decir el Kuntur de Urin y el Anga de Hanan, su espíritu continuamente se abonada en las venas de los Runas

4

93

THE MEETING OF THE CONDOR OF URIN
AND THE EAGLE OF HANAN

de este Continente.

Su fuerza motivó a que el norte y el sur se unan; la unión de la gente del Norte con el Sur significaba también la unión del Cóndor y del Aguila. El Cóndor y el Aguila se unieron juntando sus lágrimas desde Jahanpacha (cielo) y Ucupacha (subsuelo). De esta unión brotó centru américa, en este trozo de tierra se concentró la sabiduría de Hanan y de Urín y se desarrollaron nuevas naciones, cuyos pobladores tuvieron la capacidad de sembrar la tierra en medio del gran océano y convertirlo a esto en lo que hoy es centro-américa.

Estos pueblos orientados por las leyes de Allpa Mama y Pacha Mama, tuvieron que atravesar situaciones difíciles, una de ellas fue la descuartización de sus naciones. Al producirse esta tragedia, los Willak Umus instruyeron a sus Amautas, Curacas, Arawikus... etc, a crear profecías que orienten o guíen a nuestros pueblos. Estas profecías debían enseñar a las naciones indias a mantenerse sólidas, unidas y sobre todo, a buscar los caminos más adecuados para su liberación.

La iniciación de la liberación de los pueblos indios se simbolizaría con diferentes profecías, una de ellas, es la unión de las lágrimas de Cóndor de Urín y del Aguila de Hanan. La unión de estas de estas lágrimas soldarán nuestras heridas, fortalecerán el espíritu, el cuerpo y el pensamiento. El gran espíritu abrirá surcos. En cada surco regará su semilla, y en cada paso brotarán batallones de hombres que expondrán sus pechos para rechazar las dagas del enemigo; extenderán sus manos para borrar la opresión, la explotación y la injusticia y escribirán en la gran hoja del cielo la sagrada palabra de Libertad.

La unión del Cóndor y del Aguila según la profecía debe producirse en este quinto siglo. El quinto siglo nacerá con nuevo espíritu. Este espíritu nuevo unirá nuevamente a las naciones indias del norte, centro y sud-américa.

5

EL ENCUENTRO DEL CONDOR DE URIN Y EL AGUILA DE HANAN

En el desarrollo de la vida de las Naciones Indias, cada cinco siglos se producen transformaciones de fondo y de forma. Estos cambios no pierden su esencia, van recubriéndose de nueva piel, la vieja se rejuvenece, se nutre de pura energía. Esta energía es transmitida por los grandes espíritus de la Allpa Mama y la Pacha Mama; es decir, de la naturaleza y del Universo en general.

Hace miles de años, cuando la vida inició su ciclo vital, Pachakamak (Dios del tiempo) creó a Inti (sol) y a Quilla (luna), de la unión de sus lágrimas y procreó a los Runas, a los hombres de este continente Appia –Yala (América). De la unión de Inti y de Quilla se desbordó la vida, en este parto brotó el Cóndor y el aguila; es decir el Kuntur de Urín y el Anga de Hanan, su espíritu continuamente se abonada en las venas de los Runas

4

In the unfolding of the life of the Indian Nations, every five centuries produces transformations of both foundations and forms. With these changes, life does not lose its essence. It becomes covered with new skin. The old is rejuvenated. It is nourished with pure energy. This energy is transmitted by the great spirits of Allpa Mama and Pacha Mama, that is, of nature and of the Universe, in general.

Thousands of years ago, when life initiated its vital cycle, Pachakamak (God of Time) created Inti (the sun) and Quilla (the moon) out of the union of its tears and, thus, gave birth to the Runas, to the people of this continent Abya Yala and in this birth emerged the Condor and the Eagle, the Kuntur of Urin and the Anga de Hanan, their spirits continually enriching the veins of the Runas of this continent.

94

Their strength motivated the north and south to unite. The union of the people of the North with the South also signifies the union of the Condor and the Eagle. The Condor and the Eagle joined their tears from Jahanpacha (the sky) to Ucupacha (the underground). Out of this union sprang Central America. In this piece of earth was concentrated the wisdom of Hana and Urin. New nations developed, whose inhabitants had the capacity to sow the earth in the middle of a great ocean and convert it into what is today Central America.

These peoples, oriented by the laws of Allpa Mama and Pacha Mama, had to pass through difficult situations, one of which was the splitting of its nations into four parts. After this tragedy, the Willak Umus (prophets) instructed their Amautas, Curacas, Arawikus or wise men to create prophecies that would orient and guide our peoples. These prophecies would teach the Indian nations to maintain themselves solid, united and, above all, to search for the most appropriate paths for their liberation.

The beginning of the liberation of the Indian people would be symbolized by different prophecies, one of which is the union of the tears of the Condor of Urin and the Eagle of Hanan. The union of these tears would cauterize our wounds and fortify our spirit, body and thought. The great spirit would open furrows and in each furrow would water its seed, and in each step would spring battalions of men who would bare their chests to fend off the daggers of the enemy. They would reach out with their hands to erase oppression, exploitation and injustice, and they would write on the huge page of the sky the sacred word of liberty.

The union of the Condor and Eagle, according to the prophecy, should occur in this century. The fifth century will be born with a new spirit. This new spirit will unite once again the Indian nations of North, Central and South America.

•

The Encuentro began at the CONAIE office in Quito with a press conference. The international media was there in force, the notable exception being the US press. Berkeley was the only city to be represented at the Encuentro, and the mayor's message was extremely well received.

The Encuentro was officially opened at the National Congress, in a hall next door to where the Ecuadorean legislators met. It was packed with well over a thousand people. On the wall behind the podium was a gigantic banner written partly in Quichua, partly in Spanish: "The struggle for land is the sovereignty of Latin America. 1992: not one more hacienda in Ecuador!" The proceedings were bilingual, a simultaneous English translation available on headphones. The upstairs floors were swarming with police in riot gear. A group of musicians from Ota Valo, a town in the mountains, in dark felt hats, a long braid hanging down behind, played rousing Andean music with guitars, flutes, panpipes, drums, and horns. Cristobal Tapuy, the president of CONAIE opened the proceedings, followed by leaders from many different countries, each focusing on the specific struggles for survival and self-determination in their areas. Cayuqueo spoke for Mapuches of Argentina; María Toj of the Comite de Unidad Campesinos spoke for Highland Mayas of Guatemala; Earen Tapiz Villegas spoke for Mexico. At the end Rose Auger, Cree from Canada, performed a beautiful ceremonial prayer.

[Photos by John Curl][14]

Other SAIIC people soon arrived, including Xihuanel Huerta (ChicanIndia), Yolanda Ronquillo, Guillermo Delgado (Quechua, Bolivia), Gina Pacaldo (San Carlos Apache/Chicana).

Altogether from the US and Canada were around 70 Native people and around 30 non-Natives.

CONAIE (Confederación de Nacionalidades Indígenas del Ecuador), the host organization, represented all of the indigenous nationalities of the country, some organized into provincial organizations, and others not. CONAIE was created in 1986 out of the union of two already existing regional organizations, ECUARUNARI (Confederación Kichwa del Ecuador), representing the highlands, formed over 20 years earlier, and CONFENIAE (Confederación de Nacionalidades Indígenas de la Amazonía Ecuatoriana) representing the Ecuadorian Amazon, formed in 1980.

97

People poured into Quito from all over the hemisphere, a vast variety of faces, over 400 people from 120 different Indian nations, tribes and organizations.

The conference workshops each produced resolutions that they brought to the final plenary, where a series of specific proposals were agreed to. The main points were put into a document called the Declaration of Quito, which everyone present signed at the end of the conference. It begins with reflections, and continues with affirmations:

> Based on these aforementioned reflections, the organizations united in the First Continental Gathering of Indigenous Peoples reaffirm:
>
> **1. Our emphatic rejection of the Quincentennial celebration, and the firm promise that we will turn that date into an occasion to strengthen our process of continental unity and struggle towards our liberation.**

The Declaration continues with a series of affirmations: An international Peoples' Tribunal will be constituted to judge the 1492 invasion. Indemnification should be paid to the Indian peoples. The United Nations should declare the right of self-determination of indigenous peoples. "Our definitive liberation can only express itself as the full exercise of our self-determination... Without Indian self-government and control of our lands, autonomy cannot exist." A campaign should be undertaken against the transnational corporations that are despoiling indigenous lands. The 500 Years Campaign should be constituted in national committees, with full participation of non-Indian "popular sectors", and continental coordination. The US delegates were asked to make these questions into electoral issues.

"We demand respect for our right to life, to land, to free organization and expression of our culture... We affirm our decision to defend our culture, education and religion as fundamental to our identity as Peoples, reclaiming and maintaining our own forms of spiritual life and communal coexistence, in an intimate relationship with our Mother Nature... A new pluralist, democratic and humane society, in which peace is guaranteed, should be constructed."

The Quito Gathering ended with a call for future Encuentros, the next possibly in Guatemala.

The full Declaration of Quito is in Appendix E, page 195. An Oral History of the Encuentro is in Appendix D, page 164.

Declaration of Quito

Indigenous Alliance of the Americas on 500 Years of Resistance, July 1990

The Continental Gathering "500 Years of Indian Resistance," with representatives from 120 Indian Nations, International and Fraternal organizations, met in Quito, Ecuador on July 17-20, 1990. The gathering was organized by the Confederation of Indian Nations of Ecuador (CONAIE), the Organization of Indian Nations of Colombia (ONIC) and SAIIC. The following is the Declaration from this gathering. To order the English translation of the conference resolutions, please send a five dollar contribution to SAIIC. The North, South and Meso-American conference participants declare before the world the following:

We Indians of America have never abandoned our constant struggle against the conditions of oppression, discrimination and exploitation which were imposed upon us as a result of the European invasion of our ancestral territories.

Our stuggle is not a mere conjunctural reflection of the memory of 500 years of oppression which the invaders, in complicity with the "democractic" governments of our countries, want to turn into events of jubilation and celebration. Our struggle as Indian People, Nations and Nationalities is based on our identity, which shall lead us to true liberation. We are responding aggressively, and commit ourselves to reject this "celebration."

The struggle of our People has acquired a new quality in recent times. This struggle is less isolated and more organized. We are now completely conscious that our total liberation can only be expressed through the complete exercise of our self-determination. Our unity is based on this fundamental right. Our self-determination is not just a simple declaration.

We must guarantee the necessary conditions that permit complete exercise of our self-determination; and this, in turn must be expressed as complete autonomy for our Peoples. Without Indian self-government and without control of our territories, there can be no autonomy.

The achievement of this objective is a principal task for Indian Peoples however, through our struggles we have learned that our problems are not different, in many repects, from those of other popular sectors. We are convinced that we must march alongside the peasants, the workers, the marginalized sectors, together with intellectuals committed to our cause, in order to destroy the dominant system of oppression and construct a new society, pluralistic, democratic and humane, in which peace is guaranteed.

The existing nation states of the Americas, their constitutions and fundamental laws are judicial/political expressions that negate our socio-economic, cultural and political rights.

At this point in our struggle, one of our priorities is to demand a complete structural change which allows for the recognition of Indian people's rights to self-determination, and the control of our territories through our own governments.

Our problems will not be resolved through the self-serving politics of governmental entities which seek integration and ethno-development. It is necessary to have an integral trasformation at the level of the state and national society; that is to say, the creation of a new nation.

In this Gathering it has been clear that territorial rights are a fundamental demand of the Indigenous Peoples of the Americas. Based on these aforementioned reflections, the organizations united in the First Continental Gathering of Indigenous Peoples reaffirm:

1. Our emphatic rejection of the Quincentennial celebration, and the firm promise that we will turn that date into an occasion to strengthen our process of continental unity and struggle towards our liberation.

2. Ratify our resolute political project of self-determination and our autonomy, in the framework of nation states, under a new political order, with respect for whatever forms of organization each Nation determines appropriate for their situation.

3. Affirm our decision to defend our culture, education, and religion as fundamental to our identity as Peoples, reclaiming and maintaining our own forms of spiritual life and communal coexistence, in an intimate relationship with our Mother Earth.

4. We reject the manipulation of organizations which are linked to the dominant sectors of society and have no Indigenous representation, who usurp our name for (their own) imperialist interests. At the same time, we affirm our choice to strengthen our own organizations, without excluding or isolating ourselves from other popular struggles.

5. We recognize the important role that Indigenous women play in the struggles of our Peoples. We understand the necessity to expand women's participation in our organizations and we reaffirm that it is one struggle, men and women together, in our liberation process, and a key question in our political practices.

6. We Indian Peoples consider it vital to defend and conserve our natural resources, which right now are being attacked by transnational corporations. We are convinced that this defense will be realized if it is Indian People who administer and control the territories where we live, according to our own principles of organization and communal life.

7. We oppose national judicial structures which are the result of the process of colonization and neo-colonization. We seek a New Social Order that embraces our traditional exercise of Common Law, an expression of our culture and forms of organization. We demand that we be recognized as Peoples under International Law, and that this recognition be incorporated into the respective Nation States.

8. We denounce the victimization of Indian People through violence and persecution, which constitutes a flagrant violation of human rights. We demand respect for our right to life, to land, to free organization and expression of our culture. At the same time we demand the release of our leaders who are held as political prisoners, an end to repression, and restitution for the harms caused us.

Declaration of Quito, July, 1990

100

•

ENCUENTRO VIDEO

SAAIC made a video of the Encuentro, with the narrative in Spanish and featuring an English interview with Rose Auger, the spiritual leader of the Encuentro (who passed peacefully in 2006). You can watch it on YouTube at

http://youtube/X8_x25qC2VY

•

Among the Participants
at the Encuentro

Among attendees were Rupert Robinson, leader of a Maroon colony on Jamaica; Irvince Auguiste, from a Carib settlement on the island of Dominica. June Le Grande, Cherokee storyteller, with a radio show on KKUP Cupertino, California; Elena, a translator; Agnes, who had a Sonoma County radio show; her teenaged daughter Sunshine; Alfredo Quarto, who organized a political caravan called the Chautauqua. Several Alliance for Cultural Democracy (ACD) people arrived, Joe Lambert of Life on the Water Theater at Fort Mason in San Francisco, and Larry Rinder of the U.C. Berkeley Art Museum. NGOs and academics were strongly represented: Paul Haible, from the Vanguard Foundation, Juan Alista from Oxfam, Gretchen Kaapcke, Pedro Almeida, Virginia Tilley from EAFORD, Eric from Arctic to Amazon Alliance. Others from the north included Sarah James, Gwich'in from Arctic Village Alaska; Roy Crazy Horse, from the Powhatan Renape nation; Eugene Hazgood, (Diné-Navajo) involved with Big Mountain; Albert Bender (Cherokee), an attorney; Ray Williams from the Swinomish tribe in Washington; Jackie Warledo (Seminole); the poets Joy Harjo (Muskogee) and Patricia Blanco (Chicana); Luz Guerra from Boriquen (Puerto Rico); Cindi Alvitre, (Gabrieleña); Robert Allen Warrior (Osage); Tupac Enrique Acosta (Nahua/Xicano) from Phoenix.

Among the local leaders and coordinators of the Encuentro were Cristobal Tapuy (Quichua, President of CONAIE); Luis Macas (Quichua, future president of CONAIE); vice-president Rafael Pandam (Shuar); Luis Vargas (Achuar, president of CONFENIAE); Luisa Chongo, Rosa Vacacela (Sarguro), José Almeida (CONAIE); Mecho Calderón and Manuel Imbaquinga (ECUARUNARI); and Victor Hugo Jijón (CDDH-Comisión por la Defensa de los Derechos Humanos).

CHAPTER FOUR

BARIA and Resistance 500

"How to re-educate world opinion effectively:

1. Declare and reaffirm October 12, 1992 as International Day of Solidarity with Indigenous People."

> Resolution of the All-Native Indigenous Conference, D-Q / 1992 All Peoples Network Conference

•

The third Native conference that played a pivotal role in Indigenous Peoples Day was the All-Native Indigenous Conference at D-Q University, in Davis, California, which on its final day moved to Oakland's Laney College, where it was opened to include nonNative people and became the 1992 All Peoples Network Conference.

When the participants at the Encuentro arrived back in their home communities from Ecuador, they found numerous people anxious to hear about the Quito gathering, and energetically preparing for the counter-quincentennial. As they had promised in Quito, each reported back to their local compañeras and compañeros, and with them began to gear up for the coming 500 year commemoration. Over the following months almost every progressive cultural and social justice organization in the Bay Area region, Native and non-Native, came together into the counter-quincentennial coalition known as Resistance 500.

Shortly after the Encuentro, a meeting was held in the Berkeley mayor's office, between Mayor Hancock, Nilo Cayuqueo (director of SAIIC, a central organizer of the Encuentro), John Curl (Hancock's representative to the Encuentro), and two people Nilo brought, Antonio Gonzales and Millie Ketcheshawno. Tony (Seri/Chicano) was director of the International Indian Treaty Council (IITC); Millie (Muscogee) had played an important role in the Alcatraz Island occupation of 1969-1971, and had been the first woman director of Inter-Tribal Friendship House in Oakland (a primary center for the Bay Area Indian community). Neither had attended the Quito conference; both would play important roles in the events to follow.

As mentioned in the previous chapter, the Native groups that organized the Quito conference were all from Latin America. Historical experiences of life under the different colonial powers had taken different forms of oppression for Native people. While the Encuentro's goal was to bridge north-south differences, the conference tried to sidestep organizational problems by having all US and Canadian people attend as individuals, not as organizational representatives.

But back here in the Bay Area things were different. Nilo understood that everyone had to work in coalition, starting with SAIIC and the Northern Native nations' progressive organizations.

At the meeting in the mayor's office, Cayuqueo and Curl reported about the Quito Encuentro. Ketcheshawno and Gonzales already knew about it, since word had spread quickly in the Indigenous community. Then the five brainstormed about how to proceed.

Mayor Hancock suggested that we needed to get the city to set up an official "task force" to study the issues and report findings and recommendations. First we would need to thread our way through the city processes of boards and commissions. The most important bodies would be the Peace and Justice Commission and the School Board. If we could garner their support, they would report to the city council, and that would open the door to the council setting us up as an official task force. Loni offered to find us a space in city hall to work out of, if we needed it.

Treaty Council at the UN

The International Indian Treaty Council, which had originated the idea of Indigenous Peoples Day in 1977, brought it back to the United Nations again in 1990.

Earlier that year, at the same time as Cayuqueo and SAIIC had been organizing the Encuentro, Tony Gonzales and ITTC had been busy in New York City at the UN Economic and Social Council (ECOSOC) session of May 1-25, 1990, lobbying for the UN to declare 1992 the International Year of Indigenous Peoples, to declare October 12 to be International Indigenous Peoples Day, and to declare the next decade the International Decade of the World's Indigenous Peoples. Tony and the IITC met with intense opposition from the US government and other sources. The governments didn't want any interference with the 1992 Columbus "Jubilee."

The result was that the UN General Assembly proclaimed 1993 (not 1992) the International Year of the World's Indigenous People. They intentionally made it *people* instead of *peoples* to avoid recognizing them as tribal nations. The governments would not touch October 12, and finally in 1994 declared the arbitrary date of August 9 to be International Day of the World's Indigenous People and 1995–2005 to be the International Decade of the World's Indigenous People.

However, the governments could not derail the movement to celebrate October 12 as Indigenous Peoples Day in place of a celebration of Columbus's colonial and imperialist enterprise.

•

Report Back and Slide Show

The first public informational event about the Encuentro that SAIIC put on in the Bay Area, cosponsored by the Alliance for Cultural Democracy (the multicultural activist arts group), was a Report Back and slide show that we presented six times in Berkeley, Oakland, San Francisco, and San Jose in August and September, 1990. It included an historical section of 16th century images of the Taino Indians and Columbus's attacks on them. Bobsy Draper and others contributed slides from photos from the Encuentro. The events were well attended.

D-Q All-Native Conference
Bay Area Regional Indian Alliance (BARIA)

The Quito Encuentro had resolved to turn October 12 "into an occasion to strengthen our process of continental unity and struggle towards our liberation." The D-Q All-Native Indigenous Conference took the critical next step, and resolved to turn that date into Indigenous Peoples Day.

In October 1990 SAIIC organized a meeting in Minneapolis, Minnesota, of North American Native activists as a follow-up to the Encuentro. There they decided to call a major North American region (US/Canada) all-Indian conference at D-Q University in Davis, California, to be followed by a one-day meeting in the Bay Area with non-Indian people to develop strategies and to network together toward a unified action plan for 1992.

North American Conference on 500 Years of Resistance

The *1992 Bay Area Regional Indian Alliance* is coordinating an *All-Native Conference* to plan and coordinate *1992 Year of Indigenous Peoples* activities. The conference is an important North American follow-up to the July 1990 international gathering in Quito, Ecuador and the October 1990 meeting in Minneapolis.

The gathering will be held Friday through Sunday, March 22-24, 1991 at DQ University, a private, fully accredited Indian-sanctioned college, located 8 miles west of Davis, California. Papers, draft statements, action plans, recommendations, or suggestions should be submitted by March 18, 1991. Delegates from Indian organizations planning 500 Years activities as well as interested Indian people from the US and Canada are invited. If you are planning to attend, be sure to contact the coordinators as soon as possible.

For more information contact:
All Native Conference
DQ University
PO Box 409
Davis, California 95617
Telephone: (916) 758-0470

Abya Yala News (SAIIC)

107

The all-Indian conference was scheduled for March 22-24, 1991. The follow-up one-day conference with nonIndian people was to take place the next day, at Laney College in Oakland. To host the D-Q All-Native Indigenous Conference, they formed a coordinating group called the 1992 Bay Area Regional Indian Alliance (BARIA).

D–Q University was a two-year Indian college founded in 1975 near Davis, California. The full name of the school was usually not spelled out because D stands for the name of the Iroquois Great Peacemaker, and many Haudenosaunee believe his name should be spoken only in a spiritual context. The Q stands for Quetzalcoatl, the Plumed Serpent of Indigenous Mexico. The D-Q name is a recognition of the north/south unity of all American Indigenous peoples.

On March 22, over one hundred North American Indian representatives came together at D-Q, and consolidated the fruits of months of intense organizing in their communities. The main organizers were SAIIC, IITC, Inter-Tribal Friendship House, Seventh Generation Fund, and the Santa Clara Indian Valley Council. The conference divided into six work commissions: Action plan for 1992 and beyond; Indian prisoners and freedom of religion; Environment; Education; Communication and Media; Respect and care of Indian families and children.

•

At the end of three days of discussions, the All-Native Indigenous Conference resolved:

HOW TO RE-EDUCATE WORLD OPINION EFFECTIVELY
1. Declare and reaffirm October 12, 1992 as International Day of Solidarity with Indigenous People.

•

HOW TO RE-EDUCATE WORLD OPINION EFFECTIVELY

1. Declare and re-affirm Oct. 12, 1992 as Int'l Day of Solidarity with Indigenous Peoples

2. Network with support groups

3. Send delegates to Mexico's 500 year committee meeting (5/91)

4. Call on commission for delegates to attend the signing of the declaration for Indigenous peoples rights in N.Y.C. (10/12/92)

5. Concept paper to be submitted at next regional conference

6. Encourage networking with progressive international and environmental organizations.

7. We will advocate for treaty rights and non-treaty indigenous nations

8. Encourage legislation that liberalizes border crossing - we do not recognize borders

9. We encourage border conferences

10. We join in support of no consumption, no purchases on Oct 13 *1992*

11. We call on the U.N. to sponsor a conference specifically on 92-93 activities for indigenous peoples

12. We encourage D.Q. to be a clearing house of curriculum education for public institutions for all grade levels

13. Organize a meeting with int'l funding sources ie. churches, foundations to include indigenous representatives on how they can help with the 500 year campaign

14. Encourage the development of a ten year plan by the 500 year committee

15. Communicate to the Pope our indigenous point of view on the 500 year commemoration

16. Co-ordinate common dates in which indigenous peoples can join together in common effort such as quarterly at season changes, similar to Earth day

17. Purchase full page newspaper ads for support of our struggle

18. We encourage the videotaping of this strategy session of the '92 conference to be distributed nationally and int'ly as a learning tool

19. Call to the churches to apologize, join in the oppositions to the celebrations and support the opposition with resources.

20. Call on the European Common Market not to invest in Latin American countries. where governments are violating Indian rights.

21. We call to the European support groups to organize a campaign of education and support to the 500 Years of Indigenous Resistence.

22. We agree to network through the continent setting up clearing houses.

23. Restriction of landing of the three ships Santa Maria, La Nina and La Pinta coming to our continent without permission.

1992 All People's Network Conference

The atmosphere was charged in Oakland's Laney College Forum on March 25, 1991, as over 100 Indian delegates from across North America met with over 200 nonIndian environmentalists, educators, artists, media people, and a wide variety of progressives, human rights activists, and cultural workers at the 1992 All People's Network Conference.

The invitation to the All Peoples Conference stated that the mission of the event was "to form a broad coalition of all peoples in order to counter the official 'Encounter' of Two Worlds or 'The Discovery of America.'"

> The purpose of the conference is to develop an action plan and strategize for October 1992. The suggested agenda will include workshops on Education, Media, Cultural and Art Activities, Legislation, and Environment. We are calling on all sectors of society to form an alliance to demand that governments, religious institutions and educational institutions tell the truth about what took place 500 years ago and examine how these injustices continue today. We welcome your suggestions for the agenda.

The conference sponsors were SAIIC, IITC, ACD, the National Chicano Human Rights Council, the Chasky, and the African People's Revolutionary Party.

At this conference a number of people got involved who would go on to play important roles in Berkeley's Indigenous Peoples Day.

Millie Ketcheshawno was there with Dennis Jennings, a Sac and Fox man who had been with her on Alcatraz during the 1969-1971 occupation, and later worked for IITC before Tony Gonzales became director. With Dennis and Millie were Bernadette Zambrano and Lakota Hardin; Gabriel Hernandez and Ariana Montes, from the National Chicano Human Rights Council and the Chicano Moratorium; Dorinda Moreno, organizer for the Peace and Dignity Journeys; and Nina Serrano, poet and radio host with a show on KPFA .

1992 All People's Network Conference
Laney College Forum
900 Fallon Street, Oakland, California
Monday, March 25, 1991
9:00 am to 6:00 pm

We extend this invitation to all organizations and people interested in participating in the **1992 All People's Network Conference.**

In July, 1990, a continental Indian Conference on the 500 years of European invasion took place in Quito, Ecuador. About 70 Indian delegates and 30 non-Indian people from North America attended this conference. At a follow-up meeting in October, 1990, in Minneapolis, Minnesota, it was decided to call for a North American (including Canada and Alaska) Regional meeting in California in March, 1991. An all-Indian meeting will take place at DQ University in Davis, California on March 22 - 24, 1991. Many people understand that there is a need to form a broad coalition of all peoples in order to counter the official "Encounter of Two Worlds" or "The Discovery of America." Most of the Indian delegates have expressed the desire to meet with non-Indian peoples to develop strategies and network together to organize a unified action plan for 1992. This conference on March 25 will be the opportunity for this meeting to take place.

The purpose of the conference is to develop an action plan and strategize for October 1992. The suggested agenda will include workshops on Education, Media, Cultural and Art Activities, Legislation, and Environment. We are calling on all sectors of society to form an alliance to demand that governments, religious institutions and eductional institutions tell the truth about what took place 500 years ago and examine how these injustices continue today. We welcome your suggestions for the agenda.

The registration fee of $10.00 will include breakfast and lunch. Travel expenses and lodging accomodations are not included, however, we are trying to find places to stay for those who will need it. You can register by contacting IITC or SAIIC. We are looking forward to seeing you on March 25, 1991, at Laney College.

1992 All People's Network Conference sponsors: The International Indian Treaty Council (IITC) the South and Meso American Indian Information Center (SAIIC   the Alliance for Cultural Democracy, the All African People's Revolutionary Party, the Chasky and the National Chicano Human Rights Council.

For more info: IITC, 710 Clayton Street, #1, San Francisco, CA 94117, (415) 566-0251 (FAX 415 - 566 - 0442), or SAIIC, 1212 Broadway #830, Oakland, CA, 94612 (415) 843-4263 (FAX 415-843-4264).

Lee Sprague, Potawatomi from Michigan, member of the Little River Bank of Ottawa Indians, brought a set of architectural plans for what he called the Turtle Island Monument, a large sculpture of a turtle surrounded by plaques with the names of Native nations, and beneath it, a time capsule. The architect, Marlene Watson, Diné (Navajo), was also there. Turtle Island is the American continent. According to Lee, there was no monument to Native people in this country, so he was gathering support to have it built, and he had heard that Berkeley might be a possible place.

South & Meso American Indian Information Center (SAIIC)
1212 Broadway #830 Oakland, California 94612
Telephone: (415) 834-4263 Fax: (415) 834-4264 Electronic mail: Peacenet (cap: SAIIC)

RELEASE DATE: March 21, 1991

PRESS CONFERENCE
at the
ALL PEOPLE'S NETWORK CONFERENCE
ON 500 YEARS OF RESISTANCE 1492 - 1992

WHAT: Indian delegates from across North America will be gathering in the Bay Area to confer with people concerned with organizing a response to official plans for the Quincentenary of Columbus' first voyage. The Bay Area will be the international focus of the planned celebration, when replicas of Columbus' three ships, having sailed from Spain, will enter the Golden Gate on October 12, 1992. Many people feel that a gala celebration is inappropriate and that this is an opportunity for people to reflect on the last 500 years of colonization of the American Continent. The aim of the conference is to develop strategies and organize a unified action plan for the counter-commemoration of the 1992 Jubilee.

An all-Indian conference on the same topic is taking place from March 22nd to the 24th at DQ University in Davis. Many delegates from the DQ Conference will be participating in the All People's Network Conference.

WHEN: Monday, March 25, 10:00 - 10:30 am

WHERE: Laney College Forum
  900 Fallon Street (Across from Kaiser Convention Center), at Lake Meritt BART
  Oakland

CONFERENCE SCHEDULE
- 9:00 - 9:30 am Opening Ceremony by June LeGrand
    (outdoors, weather permitting)
- 9:30 - 10:00 Keynote remarks by Nilo Cayuqueo and Wilson Riles, Jr.

- 10:00 - 10:30 • Press conference.

- 10:30 - 12:30 Workshops: Education; Media; 1992 Actions and Activities.
- 12:30 - 1:45 Lunch
- 1:45 - 3:45 Workshops: Legislation; the Environment; Culture and Art.
- 4:00 - 6:00 Plenary

CONTACT: Karl Erb or Peter Veilleux
South & Meso American Indian Information Center
1212 Broadway, Room 830
Oakland, CA 94612
Tel: (415) 834-4263
Fax: (415) 834-4264

Two nonNative people who would be important members of the Berkeley committee got involved at this conference, Mark and Nancy Gorrell. Both were active in the Berkeley Ecology Center and in Berkeley Citizens Action, the local progressive coalition.

The conference opened with a ceremony of burning sage, led by two spiritual leaders who had attended the Quito Encuentro: June Le Grande and Ed Burnstick.

June was also the keynote speaker: "We need to bring out the truths of history and of the present, for the sake of all the unborn generations," Le Grande said. "We've got to educate the educators. Our schools need to teach the facts, not the falsehoods that fill many of the books today."[15]

Inspired speeches by SAIIC director Nilo Cayuqueo, Oakland Councilmember Wilson Riles, Jr., and Betty Kano, National Coordinator of ACD, detailed how the invasion that Columbus led caused devastation to Indian civilizations, and how this oppression continues today.

"After all the destruction and violations of human rights, repression of indigenous people and devastation to the earth," Cayuqueo said, "they are trying to impose a New World Order, which for us is the same order of oppression we have been suffering under for 500 years. We need to say 'no' to the official celebration."

Betty Kano added, "The 500 Years of Resistance challenges us to struggle together against the New World Order and to work together for the future of the planet for the next 500 years."

Riles, a leader in the Bay Area Free South Africa Movement, proposed that the Quincentennial get back to the original meaning of the Biblical word "Jubilee," which signified that every fifty years all land would revert to its original owners and all debts would be forgiven.

At the press conference that followed, Tony Gonzales explained, "The D-Q gathering planned major events on behalf of our ancestors, those that have gone before us. And it is from this spiritual and inspired position that we will move the agenda forward for 1992 and beyond, all for the love of our coming generations."

We spent most of the rest of the day in workshops, three in the morning and three in the afternoon. The morning workshops were: 1992 Activities, Actions and Networking; Media; and Education. In the afternoon were Legislation; Environment; Culture and Art. Each workshop developed an action plan for its area of discussion.

Then at 4:15 each workshop reported back to the plenary.

After hearing all the reports and recommendations, the plenary basically affirmed and consolidated the most important resolutions of the earlier All-Native Conference at D-Q:

1992 All People's Network Conference

DQ University, March 1991

1. Declare and reaffirm October 12, 1992 as International Day of Solidarity with Indigenous Peoples.

2. Advocate for treaty rights and non-treaty indigenous Nations.

3. Encourage legislation that liberalizes border crossing. We do not recognize borders.

4. Join in support of no energy or material consumption on October 13, 1992.

5. Call on the United Nations to sponsor a conference on 1992-1993 activities for indigenous peoples.

6. Communicate to the Pope our indigenous point of view regarding the 500 year commemoration.

7. Coordinate common dates in which indigenous peoples can join together in a common effort, for example, quarterly at season changes (similar to Earth Day).

8. Call to the Churches to apologize and support an indigenous perspective of 1992.

9. Call on the European Common Market to not invest in Latin American countries where governments are violating human rights.

10. Demand the restriction of landing of the three ships, the Nina, the Pinta and the Santa Maria.

Source: *500 Years of Resistance; 1992 International Directory and Resource Guide.* Oakland: South and Meso-American Indian Information Center (SAIIC), p. 11.

The universal consensus was to form a new organization to carry on the work of the coalition. The Diné (Navajo) elders in attendance said we needed to include the word "Resistance" and the number "500" in our name. Thus we became Resistance 500.

We empowered the conference organizers to proceed with follow-up meetings leading to actions. We divided the Bay Area into five task force areas: San Francisco, Oakland, Berkeley, San Jose, and Other. Almost everyone signed up to join a task force. So at the end of deliberations a new all-people coalition emerged on March 25, 1991, Resistance 500, with a plan for leading coordinated actions to counter the officially planned "Jubilee" commemoration of Columbus's invasion.

Each local Resistance 500 task force began to hold meetings, and once a month we all came together at Inter-Tribal Friendship House in Oakland, to report on our progress, exchange ideas, and coordinate efforts.

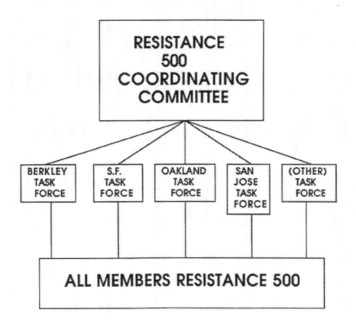

The Bay Area urban Indian community's roots went back to the 1950s when large numbers of Native people from all over the US were lured off reservations and rural areas and brought here with promises of jobs by the Bureau of Indian Affairs' Relocation Program, which was connected to their "termination" policy of disbanding all tribes by withdrawing recognition. Most of the early community were young single people and young families. West coast cities were focuses of the program, and the Bay Area wound up with one of the highest urban concentrations of American Indian populations in the nation. Indian people from many tribes, reservations and rural areas adjusted to urban living by creating a network linked by culture and shared experiences.

Resistance 500!
"Organizing for 1992 & Beyond"

PO Box 28703, Oakland, California 94604
Telephone: 415-834-4263   Fax: 415-834-4264

July 16, 1991

Agenda

I.   Call To Order

II.   Invocation

III.   Introductions

IV.   Review/Revise/Approve Agenda

V.   Review Minutes of June 24, 1991
        (Steering Committee) Coordinating Committee

VI.   Task Force/Area Program Reports   *people*

VII.   Newsletter Status   *Lee*

VIII.   Organizational Plan   *issues*
        1.   Who/What are we
        2.   Organizational Structure
        3.   Cooperative Plan   *ground rules (incl. minutes)*
                    Procedures
                    Policies
        4.   Financial functions & policies
        5.   Program Activities   *is coord. undertaking on own*
        6.   Meeting frequency

IX.   Programs and Activities Proposal/Information

X.   General Discussion

XI.   Future Meeting
        1.   Location
        2.   Time
        3.   Date
        4.   Agenda Items

XII.   Adjourn

AGENDA791

Inter-Tribal Friendship House

Inter-Tribal Friendship House (IFH), today one of the oldest urban Indian organizations in the country, became a sanctuary for the growing local Native community, a center for mutual aid and self-help, nurturing numerous people through difficult times, a gathering place for both newcomers and their descendants. The Friendship House Wednesday Night Dinner became a weekly social ritual

116

binding the community together. IFH emerged as the heart of a new, cooperative, multi-tribal Indian community. A new intertribal personal identity of "urban Indian" emerged. It was only natural that IFH became the center for Resistance 500 organizing, with the hospitality of Jim Lamenti, the director, his wife Evelyn Lamenti, Susan Lobo, Carol Wahpepah, Betty Cooper, and all the numerous IFH family. We held our meetings on Wednesday nights, after the traditional dinner.

Minutes for Resistance 500 [Steering Committee] Coordinating Committee, June 24, 1991, at Intertribal Friendship House

RESISTANCE 500

1. Composed of organizations and individuals concerned with creating 1992 campaigns/actions: networking/information dissemination.

2. GEOGRAPHIC AREA ENCOMPASSED
   - San Francisco
   - Oakland
   - Berkeley
   - San Jose

3. COMPOSITION OF DECISION-MAKING PROCESS - 50% Indian, 50% Other

4. "Steering Committee" changed to COORDINATING COMMITTEE

5. ACCOMPLISHMENTS so far
   - Meetings
       * Laney - initial formation of Resistance 500
       * SAIIC - (May)
       * IFH - (June 11)
       * IFH - (June 25)
   - Berkeley Task Force

6. IN DEVELOPMENT
   - Video Project
   - Oakland Task Force
   - San Francisco Task Force
   - Newsletter

7. NEED FOR NEXT MEETING: 7 pm JULY 16 AT IFH (Co-chairs: Millie and Jim)
   - Short synopsis of previous meetings/decisions
   - INFORMATION FROM GROUPS FOR NEWSLETTER

8. Newsletter
   A. Work Group:
   - Tom Reynolds
   - Millie K.
   - Nilak B.
   - Lee S.
   B. Purpose:
       1. Gather information from each group
       2. Calendar of Events
    1 3. Basic Resistance 500 information

Berkeley Resistance 500 Task Force

In Berkeley, our growing group continued to follow through on the plans already in progress in cooperation with Mayor Hancock, and we made presentations to different city commissions, who almost entirely greeted our efforts with enthusiasm. The Peace and Justice Commission and the School Board recommended to the Berkeley City Council to set us up as an official city citizen task force, "to develop, recommend and help implement activities for the 500 year anniversary...that present an alternative view to the traditional Eurocentric presentations of this event in ways that will involve and inform the community."

D.(c)6

CITY OF BERKELEY
CONSENT CALENDAR INFORMATION

Deadline for Council Action:

From: Commission on Peace and Justice   Date: May 21, 1991

IT IS RECOMMENDED THAT THE CITY COUNCIL: ESTABLISH A CITIZEN TASK FORCE AS A JOINT EFFORT OF THE COUNCIL AND SCHOOL BOARD TO DEVELOP, RECOMMEND AND HELP IMPLEMENT ACTIVITIES FOR THE 500 YEAR ANNIVERSARY OF COLUMBUS' FIRST VOYAGE .

1. COMMENTS, CITY ATTORNEY

   Council approval is required.

2. BACKGROUND AND NEED FOR COUNCIL ACTION:

   At the meeting of the Commission on Peace and Justice on Monday, May, 6, 1991, it was M/S/C (Ginger/Sherman) with a vote of 8-0 that the Commission recommend that the City Council establish a Citizen Task Force as a joint effort of the Council and School Board to develop, recommend and implement activities for the 500 year anniversary of Columbus' 1st voyage that conform to the Berkeley Human Rights Ordinance, the U.N. Charter, and the civil liberties guarantees in the California Constitution by presenting an alternative view to the traditionally Eurocentric presentations of this event in ways that will involve and inform the community.

   Vote: Ayes: Ginger, Sherman, Ginsburg, Lindheim, Conly, Turk, Hagen, Schwartz

   Absent: Wilkins, Haytin, Shabbas

   The U.S. Congress has set up a Columbus Quincenteary Jubilee Commission, which has selected San Francisco as the central site for America's celebration on Columbus Day October 12, 1992. The traditional and historic perspective on this event has been exclusively Eurocentric, ignoring the brutal realities of the subjugation and colonization of the indigenous peoples this expedition encountered. Community activities can be dedicated to an accurate history, recognition and celebration of our diversity, and learning from history rather than repeating it. All the residents of Berkeley of every heritage will benefit from such an alternative view.

taskfrce.con

118

[Photographer unknown]

Part of the Berkeley Resistance 500 Task Force.. L-R Back: Noele Krenkel, Dennis Jennings, John Curl, Nancy Gorrell, Anonymous. Center: Mark Gorrell, Bernadette Zambrano, Nancy Delaney, Roberto José García. Front: Patricia Lai Ching Brooks, Gabriel Hernandez, Ariana Montes

City Council Sets Up Task Force

The Berkeley City Council voted unanimously to approve the Berkeley Resistance 500 Task Force as an official city body. They empowered us to investigate the issue of the upcoming Quincentennial, and asked us make recommendations as to how the city of Berkeley should respond.

At that point our real work was just beginning. We already knew that we were going to propose replacing Columbus Day. But we needed to educate and lobby every public body in the city to gain citywide support for the idea that Indigenous Peoples Day fitted with the values of the people of Berkeley much more than a holiday celebrating Columbus.

From the beginning we decided that our group would be at least 50% Indigenous, which we generally accomplished, without ever

119

turning anyone away for that reason. We used a simple consensus decision making process, with the stipulation that on specifically Indigenous questions only Native people would be the decision makers, while non-Native people would step aside.

We elected Dennis Jennings to be the Coordinator of the first Berkeley Indigenous Peoples Day, for which we paid him a modest stipend, primarily out of a grant from the city, supplemented by small grants from the Vanguard Foundation and the Seventh Generation Fund. Dennis was our unanimous choice because of his strong leadership qualities, his organizing abilities, his dedication to social justice, his commitment to Indigenous and environmental renewal.

Mayor Hancock arranged for Dennis to work out of a desk at city hall, graciously provided by Councilmember Nancy Skinner in her office. Mark Gorrell knew how to steer our way through the city labyrinth very well from his work at the Ecology Center and as an architect, and Curl knew the city machinery from working on the West Berkeley Plan and as a member of the Berkeley Citizens Action steering committee. The Gorrells' house became our regular meeting place, and we also sometimes met at Gathering Tribes, a local center for Indigenous jewelry, crafts and art.

Although it is a town with deep progressive roots, even Berkeley has some very conservative citizens, so we knew that opposition to Indigenous Peoples Day existed. But the opposition had so little support that they never showed much of a public face.

•

Other R500 Activities

The San Francisco, Oakland, and San Jose Resistance 500 groups also lobbied their mayors and councils to set up city task forces similar to Berkeley's, but without success. Nevertheless all the groups continued moving forward together. The Resistance 500 coalition continued to hold monthly coordination meetings at Inter-Tribal Friendship House, to plan, coordinate, and carry out activities around the Bay.

It seemed like almost every progressive cultural and political group was coming on board Resistance 500. Although all were not totally coordinated, all fed energy into each other. Since the Bay Area was the scheduled center of the national Quincentennial "Jubilee" hoopla, the region also became central to the Resistance. Many events began to take shape. The counter-quincentenary movement in the Bay Area became a whirlwind of activities. Numerous groups around the Bay accomplished important and consciousness-raising activities focused on 1992.

But Berkeley was the only place which actually instituted permanent changes and became the first city in the world to get rid of Columbus Day and annually commemorate October 12 as Indigenous Peoples Day.

So by the end of October, 1992, the mission of the Berkeley Resistance 500 Task Force was over. But at the same time, the mission of the Indigenous Peoples Day Committee was just beginning.

•

Berkeley Resistance 500 Task Force

Many people participated in the Berkeley Resistance 500 Task Force that first year, and in its subsequent transformation into the Berkeley Indigenous Peoples Day Committee. Among the regulars were Dennis Jennings, Millie Ketcheshawno, Lee Sprague, Bernadette Zambrano, Gabriel Hernandez, Ariana Montes, Ken Roubideaux, Marlene Watson, Nancy Gorrell, Mark Gorrell, Bonita Sizemore, John Bellinger, Marilyn Jackson, Patricia Brooks, Roberto José García, Betty Kano, Pennie Opal, Nanette Deetz, Nancy Delaney, Les Hara, Paul Bloom, Mary Ann Wahosi, Nancy Schimmel, Diane Thomas, Eileen Baustian, Alfred Cruz, Audry Shabaas, Barbara Remick, Beth Weinberger, Beverly Slapin, Cece Weeks, Chris Clark, Cindy Senicka, Susan Lobo, Garrett Duncan, Jennifer Smith, Jos Sanchez, Judy Merriam, Lincoln Bergman, Michael Sherman, Noele Krenkel, Robert Mendoza, Regina Eisenberg, John Curl, and many more. That is just including committee members in the first two years. Numerous others were active in Resistance 500 around the Bay, including Bill Stroud, Tripp Mikich, Mat Schwartzman, Lincoln Cushing, Margo Adair, Larry Rinder, Joe Lambert, Fred Hosea, and Brian Webster.

•

CHAPTER FIVE

The First Berkeley Pow Wow, 1993

The City Council resolution of 1991 that set us up as the Berkeley Resistance 500 Task Force, included a sunset clause that our mission would be completed at the end of 1992.

Our Berkeley group made a smooth transition. After the first annual celebration, we morphed from the Resistance 500 Task Force into the Indigenous Peoples Day Committee. We remained the same core group, but now we were autonomous again.

The two main agenda topics of our first meeting after October 12, 1992, were to evaluate our events of the year, and figure out what we wanted to do for the second Indigenous Peoples Day in 1993. This was a critical crossroad.

We needed both the Berkeley community and also the larger Bay Area Native community (centered in many ways around Inter-Tribal Friendship House in Oakland) to embrace Indigenous Peoples Day for the long run, as an annual celebration, if we were to really succeed.

Millie Ketcheshawno, one of our founders, proposed that instead of another *chasky*-like cultural procession along Shattuck Avenue, we put on a pow wow in Civic Center Park. Millie had the universal respect of our group. One of the first activists on Alcatraz back in 1969, the first woman director of Inter-Tribal Friendship House, and a future filmmaker, she was Muscogee, from Oklahoma, and had come to the Bay Area in the 1950s on the BIA's Relocation Program.

The entire committee embraced the idea, so credit should properly given to the group as a whole, with Millie and others at the group's core.

Since we in the Bay Area had a strong Urban Indian population, Indigenous Peoples Day needed the local Native people to continue to embrace it if it was to survive. By celebrating Indigenous Peoples Day with a pow wow meant bringing together a pivotal meeting place for Indigenous and non-Indigenous cultures.

In 1992, as today, the Bay Area was home to one of the largest concentrations of urban Indians in North America. Around 40,000 Native Americans of many tribes and nations lived in the area, as well as 800,000 Latinos, many partly or wholly Indigenous. Today those numbers are over 50,000 Native Americans and around 1.7 million Latinos.

Millie led us into the first pow wow. If our life-affirming project of Indigenous Peoples Day was to survive, we needed to focus on positive energies, to look to the present and future, and not let our energies be drowned by the destructive forces of the past.

Lee Sprague took over from Dennis Jennings as coordinator. We asked Dennis to be our first Headman Dancer, and Millie to be our first Headwoman Dancer.

Head Staff of our first Pow Wow

MC: Roy Hopkins (Arikara)

Arena Director: Les Hara (Ponca)

Head Woman Dancer: Millie Ketcheshawno

(Mvskoke)

Head Man Dancer: Dennis Jennings (Sac and Fox)

Head Gourd Dancer: Phil Collins (Paiute)

Northern Host Drum: All Nations

Southern Host Drum: Red Hawk

Head Teen Boy: Rencho Wahpehpah

(Chippewa/Sac & Fox/Kickapoo)

Head Teen Girl: Hope Simple (Sioux)

Pow Wow Coordinator: Lee Sprague (Potawatomi)

The Roots of Pow Wows

While the roots of pow wows are very old, at the same time, pow wows as we know them today became widespread as part of the rejuvenation and resurgence of Native culture in the 1970s after the Alcatraz occupation. They became a cultural meeting place for people of many tribes and Native nations, a strong expression of the intertribal identity that Native people were forging in that era. Pow wows include dancing competitions, with prize money, and an Indian market with Native food and crafts. Pow wows are also a place where Native people welcome non-Natives, where all people of good will can come together, interact, socialize, get to know each other better, dance together, and participate in Indigenous culture.

The Bay Area's multi-tribal Native population are the heart and soul that keep the Indigenous Peoples Day Pow Wow alive and meaningful.

(For more information about pow wows, see Appendix B, on page 157.)

•

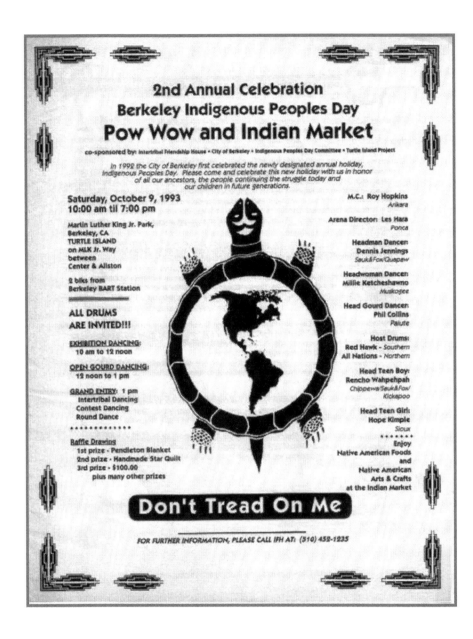

2nd Annual Celebration
Berkeley Indigenous Peoples Day
Pow Wow and Indian Market

co-sponsored by: Intertribal Friendship House • City of Berkeley • Indigenous Peoples Day Committee • Turtle Island Project

In 1992 the City of Berkeley first celebrated the newly designated annual holiday, Indigenous Peoples Day. Please come and celebrate this new holiday with us in honor of all our ancestors, the people continuing the struggle today and our children in future generations.

Saturday, October 9, 1993
10:00 am til 7:00 pm

Martin Luther King Jr. Park,
Berkeley, CA
TURTLE ISLAND
on MLK Jr. Way
between
Center & Allston

2 blks from
Berkeley BART Station

**ALL DRUMS
ARE INVITED!!!**

EXHIBITION DANCING:
10 am to 12 noon

OPEN GOURD DANCING:
12 noon to 1 pm

GRAND ENTRY: 1 pm
Intertribal Dancing
Contest Dancing
Round Dance
• • • • • • • • • • • • • •

Raffle Drawing
1st prize - Pendleton Blanket
2nd prize - Handmade Star Quilt
3rd prize - $100.00
plus many other prizes

M.C.: **Roy Hopkins**
Arikara

Arena Director: **Les Hara**
Ponca

Headman Dancer:
Dennis Jennings
Sauk&Fox/Quapaw

Headwoman Dancer:
Millie Ketcheshawno
Muskogee

Head Gourd Dancer:
Phil Collins
Paiute

Host Drums:
Red Hawk - *Southern*
All Nations - *Northern*

Head Teen Boy:
Rencho Wahpehpah
*Chippewa/Sauk&Fox/
Kickapoo*

Head Teen Girl:
Hope Kimple
Sioux
• • • • • • •
Enjoy
Native American Foods
and
Native American
Arts & Crafts
at the Indian Market

Don't Tread On Me

FOR FURTHER INFORMATION, PLEASE CALL IFH AT: (510) 452-1235

2nd Annual Celebration - Berkeley Indigenous Peoples Day
Pow Wow and Indian Market
October 9, 1993

- Schedule of Events -

9:55 a.m.	Invocation by: Diane Bower of the Yurok Nation
10:00 a.m.	Yurok Dancers
10:30 a.m.	AZTECA Dancers
11:00 a.m.	Groupo MAYA
11:30 a.m.	Hintil Dancers
12 noon	Gourd Dancing
1:00 p.m.	GRAND ENTRY
1:15 p.m.	Welcome by - Berkeley Mayor Loni Hancock
	Introduction by - Nancy Skinner
	Diane Bowers of the Yurok Nation Representative
1:30 p.m.	Round Dance honoring Berkeley City Council
2:00 p.m.	Intertribal Dancing
3:00 p.m.	Contest Dancing
5:00 p.m.	Guest Speakers
5:30 p.m.	Intertribal Dancing
6:00 p.m.	Round Dance
6:15 p.m.	Announcement of Contest Dance Winners
6:30 p.m.	Victory/Flag Dance
7:00 p.m.	END OF POW WOW

Raffle Tickets proceeds help support Indigenous Peoples Day Pow Wow & and Indian Market. Raffle Prize winners will be announced throughout the event.

1st prize - Pendleton Blanket	4th prize - Afghan made by the IFH Seniors
2nd prize - Handmade Star Quilt	5th prize - Yurok crochet bag
3rd prize - $100.00	plus many other prizes

INDIGENOUS PEOPLES DAY COMMITTEE

Greeting from Turtle Island:

Welcome to the second Annual Indigenous Peoples Day Celebration in Berkeley, Turtle Island. We gather here today to Celebrate 501 years of our Peoples survival and to honor the City of Berkeley for naming Indigenous Peoples Day in recognition of our struggles on environmental issues, sovereignty and religious expression. As Indigenous People we express our inherent rights to live by the original instructions given to us by the Creator. It is important that we share these ways of life with the majority community. We believe that this is an essential element for social progress in this hemisphere.

Last year the City of Berkeley entered into a Friendship Alliance with the Yurok Nation. This historic event is evidence of new beginnings between our Peoples and the majority community. Cultural exhanges between Yurok students and Berkeley High School students are under way - Information about Environmental Issues are being exhanged. We pray that as we move into the post-quincentennial era that you hear the voices of Indigenous Peoples. Voices that cry for freedom. Voices that have gone unheard for too long. Peace is not simply the absence of war. Peace is absolute truth and justice.

The Indigenous Peoples Day Committee works on the numerous unresolved issues between The First Nations and the majority community here on Turtle Island. We must all share the responsibility for resolving these issues for our children's future, a future where the children of the First Nations are accepted as equals and not as people under colonial rule.

We are also working on a monument dedicated to all Indigenous Nations and Peoples and our future generations here on Turtle Island.

We invite you to join the Indigenous Peoples Day Committee to work toward this future for all children. The great tree of peace began as a small seed on Turtle Island. That seed has been planted here in Berkeley. As human beings we must all work to insure its survival.

We hope you enjoy the 2nd Annual Indigenous Peoples Pow Wow and Indian Market, and we hope to see you next year.

All My Relations,

Lee A. Sprague
Indigenous Peoples Day Coordinator

P.O. BOX 2307 • BERKELEY • CALIFORNIA 94702 • (510) 464-5917

128

Watershed

We sponsored a drama, Watershed, written by Steve Most and directed by Paul Hellyer, about the Yuroks and the Salmon War of 1978, which was performed for three days before the pow wow at the Little Berkeley Theater. Performers included Jack Kohler (Yurok/) as the lead, and Nanette Deetz (Dakota/Cherokee/German), who both also visited classrooms in Berkeley High School sharing Native culture.

Recollections on "Watershed"
by Nanette Deetz

One of my most creative and enjoyable experiences was my collaboration in the play, "Watershed", a drama about the Yurok Salmon Wars of 1978, written by Stephen Most and directed by Paul Hellyer. Sponsored by the Indigenous Peoples' Day Committee, we performed the play at the Little Berkeley Theater, inside Berkeley High School, for three days before the 2nd Annual Berkeley Indigenous Peoples' Day Pow Wow in 1993. Jack Kohler, now a noted film maker/director, myself, and a small ensemble of actors and musicians performed for the public, for students, and teachers. Portions of the play were recorded and broadcast on KPFA's American Indian program. Through the medium of creative drama and music we educated and informed the non-native public about our culture, history, and existence.

We also visited classrooms at Berkeley High School, where we shared Native American culture. I played my traditional cedar bird flute and hand drum, and sang a song or two in my tribal language. We answered questions about the Salmon Wars and American Indian history and culture. Our presentations were instructive and educational for many who knew very little about tribal history and culture. Some thought we didn't exist anymore. Tribal nations are one of the least understood people by mainstream Americans, although we are also one of the most studied people.

The success of "Watershed" opened other avenues of creativity and cultural exchange for everyone involved. Jack Kohler and I collaborated musically and performed at the American Indian Film Festival in its early days at the Kaiser Convention Center in Oakland.

The arts are one of the best ways to educate and reach the minds and hearts of non-native and native community members, to stimulate conversations and true dialogs. Creative collaborations have tremendous potential to initiate constructive change. As an actor, poet, and musician, I recommend that other cities engage performing artists in similar collaborations.

Banner, Tee Shirts, Caps & Bumper Stickers

We made a 30-foot banner, which we hung across Shattuck Avenue, the central downtown street, announcing Indigenous Peoples Day to the community.

We silk-screened tee shirts and caps with the turtle logo on the front. Raffle prizes included a Pendleton blanket for first prize and a handmade star quilt for second prize.

We distributed hundreds of bumper stickers.

Berkeley's 2nd Annual

Indigenous Peoples Day

Pow Wow and Indian Market

Saturday, October 9, 1993   10:00 a.m. - 7:00 p.m., Martin Luther King Park, Berkeley Ca, TURTLE ISLAND on MLK blvd between Center & Allston

131

Pow Wow Circle

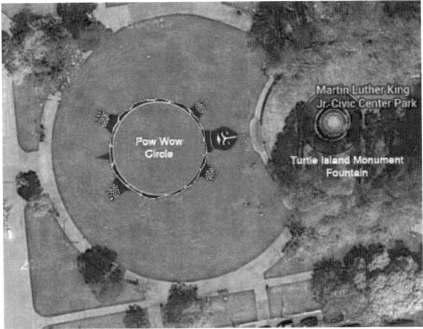

The pow wow circle in ML King, Jr. Civic Center Park, Berkeley

The morning began, as the previous year, with a sunrise ceremony at the waterfront.

Events in the park started at 10 am, with an invocation by Diane Bowers of the Yurok Nation, part of our successful campaign for a sister community relationship between Berkeley and the Yurok tribe. She was followed by exhibition dancers: first the Yuroks, then Aztec dancers, Mayan deer dancers by Grupo Maya Kusamej Junan, Hintel Pomo dancers. At noon was Gourd dancing. The Grand Entry took place at 1 pm, followed by welcoming words by Mayor Loni Hancock and others. The rest of the afternoon was contest dancing, intertribal dancing, round dancing, and guest speakers. The MC announced the contest dance winners, and the pow wow ended with a Victory/Flag Dance.

After the pow wow we staged a turkey feast in the park, and gave everyone dinner.

The First IP Day Pow Wow Picture Album

Photo from the Collection of Nancy Gorrell[16]

[*Daily Californian*, October 11, 1993]

[Photos by Nancy Gorrell]

134

138

140

For more about pow wows, see Appendix B, on page 157.

World Culture Concert

On the day after the first pow wow, Sunday, we cosponsored a World Culture Concert in Honor of Indigenous Peoples Day at Peoples' Park (across town closer to the university). Performers included All Nations Drum, Aztlan Nation (rap), Bozone (reggae), Ogi Johnson (flute) Karumata (Andean), WithOut Reservation (rap). Lee Sprague spoke. Like the pow wow, there were vendors and food booths. Cosponsors of the World Culture Concert were the Ecology Center/Farmers Market, Rock Against Racism, and Children's Light.

Turtle Logo

The turtle island logo and the eagle-condor symbol remind us of our place in the larger cultural renewal of Native people, and the gifts they bring of a consciousness that is deeply changing a world in desperate need of change. Each Indigenous Peoples Day Pow Wow contributes to that cultural renewal. Learning how to live in indigenous ways may not come easy to some people of mass-culture backgrounds, emerging from a long history of glorifying aggressive domination. But every year the pow wow offers the healing power of Native culture and its philosophy of peace, community, and sustainability.

When we transformed from Resistance 500 into the Indigenous Peoples Day Committee, we also changed our logo a little. Our first logo was the Turtle Island turtle with a map of the Americas of its shell, which we received permission to use from BARIA. When we also received permission to use the condor and eagle from the Encuentro, Marlene Watson combined the two designs into the logo that we continue to use today.

Aftermath

Most of the Bay Area groups which were active in Resistance 500 and Indigenous Peoples Day between 1990-1992, shifted their focus after 1992. The San Francisco Chasky discontinued after 1993 (then revived for a final Chasky in 2000). The Alliance for Cultural Democracy became less active and disbanded in 1996. The South and Meso-American Indian Information Center closed in 1999 after Nilo Cayuqueo, the director, returned to Argentina.

The Peace and Dignity Journeys continue every four years.

The International Indian Treaty Council/AIM-West continues to hold the annual ceremony at sunrise on Alcatraz island every October 12th.

And of course we in Berkeley continue to celebrate Indigenous Peoples Day each year.

 INDIGENOUS PEOPLES DAY

[Photos by Colleen Fawley, Hallie Frazer, & Nancy Gorrell]

Hallie Frazer, Nanette Deetz, Zulema Maixala, Marilyn Jackson (L-R)

150

Pennie Opal & Sharilane

Charlie & Nanette at Information Booth, 2016 Pow Wow

APPENDICES

APPENDIX A

Turtle Island Monument:

By Lee Sprague

The Bronze Turtle in the center of the monument symbolizes the creation of Turtle Island and sits in the center plaza. Many of the tiles have the names of Nations and Peoples who are Indigenous to Turtle Island. Many of the tiles are blank, representing the Nations and Peoples who are no longer here and the languages no longer spoken on Turtle Island.

Surrounding the center plaza, is a solar powered water fountain. The fountain symbolizes the Oceans and the Seas that surround Turtle Island, and is powered by a photo-voltaic system that uses the sun's energy to move the water over the waterfalls. The photo-voltaic system also operates the lights in the evening.

The sun's ray entering through the Turtle's eyes and nose will mark the Summer and Winter Solstices and the Spring and Fall Equinox.

Entry to the plaza is from the four directions with the main entrance from the east The people who live here on Turtle Island with us came from these four directions.

Under the Turtle is a Time Capsule to be buried for seven generations.

The inscription on the Monument/Time Capsule will say:

WE DEDICATE THIS MONUMENT TO THE SEVENTH GENERATION OF OUR CHILDREN'S CHILDREN,

WE GIVE TO YOU OUR THOUGHTS, HOPES AND DREAMS

FOR THE FUTURE OF ALL OF CREATION ON MOTHER EARTH[17]

Turtle Island Fountain

Transforming the old broken fountain into the Turtle Island Monument, first proposed by Sprague, was endorsed unanimously by the Berkeley City Council and dedicated by Native elders on the first Indigenous Peoples Day in 1992. The Fountain was conceived as a living symbol of the sustainable way of life practiced by Native People of the American continent, of the continuity between the original inhabitants of this land and the people who have come here from all corners of the globe, and as an inspiration to modern society to create a sustainable future.

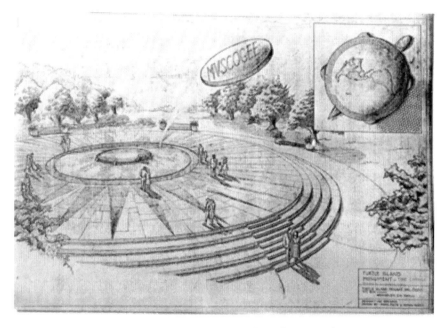

Lee Sprague/Marlene Watson

But during the city process, several civic preservationists began to lobby adamantly against the demolition of the old fountain. Finally a compromise was reached. Sprague's and Watson's original drawing had one turtle in the center of the fountain, and medallions with symbols of Native America embedded into the surrounding walkway. In the compromise, the old structure of the fountain would be

154

retained and around it turtle sculptures would be installed in the four directions with four medallions between them.

Turtle Island Monument and Time Capsule

In my people's creation stories the world was covered with water and all the animals were swimming. They were getting tired, so they respectfully asked the muskrat to go under the water to see if there was any earth. So the muskrat went down to find the earth. All of the animals were waiting for the muskrat to reappear. They were worried for the muskrat. Finally his body floated to the surface. The animals looked in his paw and they found some earth. They put the earth on the turtle's back. The rest of the animals now knew that there was earth under the water so they each went down to get some earth, first the loon then the duck and all of the rest of the animals. They all put the Earth on the turtle's back. This is how Turtle Island was created.

The Bronze Turtle in the center of the monument symbolizes the creation of Turtle Island and sits in the center plaza. Many of the tiles have the names of Nations and Peoples who are Indigenous to Turtle Island. Many of the tiles are blank, representing the Nations and Peoples who are no longer here and the languages no longer spoken on Turtle Island.

Surrounding the center plaza, is a solar powered water fountain. The fountain symbolizes the Oceans and the Seas that surround Turtle Island, and is powered by photovoltaic system that uses the sun's energy to move the water over the waterfalls. The photovoltaic system also operates the lights in the evening.

The sun's ray entering through the Turtle's eyes and nose will mark the Summer and Winter Solstices and the Spring and Fall Equinox.

Entry to the plaza is from the four directions with the main entrance from the east. The people who live here on Turtle Island with us came from these four directions.

Under the Turtle is a Time Capsule to be buried for seven generations.

The inscription on the Monument/Time Capsule will say:

WE DEDICATE THIS MONUMENT TO THE SEVENTH GENERATION OF OUR CHILDREN'S CHILDREN, WE GIVE TO YOU OUR THOUGHTS, HOPES AND DREAMS FOR THE FUTURE OF ALL OF CREATION ON MOTHER EARTH.

Indigenous Peoples Day Committee will be hosting a reception to start the fund raising campaign for the Turtle Island Monument and Time Capsule on December 4th, 1993, from 7:00 p.m. to 10:00 p.m. at the Shattuck Hotel, 2086 Allston Way, Berkeley, Turtle Island. $35.00 per person - Native American food and entertainment, RSVP (510) 464-5917.

More delays followed. In 2002, on the tenth anniversary of the original dedication, the Turtle Fountain was rededicated at the pow wow by a round dance, led by champion fancy-dancer Gilbert Blacksmith. The following spring, the City set up a Selection Committee to choose an artist and to oversee the completion of the project. The Native representatives on the committee were Sharilane

Suke (Oneida/Cherokee) and Janeen Antoine (Sicangu Lakota), both highly esteemed in the Native community. In 2005 they chose Scott Parson of South Dakota as the artist. In 2008 Parson's sculptures and medallions arrived in Berkeley. However, by that time, as the national and world economy crashed into the Great Recession, the funds to install the turtles had vanished.

[Images: the City of Berkeley]

So the turtle sculptures were put on temporary display at city hall, while the medallions remained in their packing crates in a warehouse, where they remain today, still waiting installation in their final home around the Turtle Island Fountain.

APPENDIX B

Indigenous Peoples Day & the Pow wow Highway
the new holiday & the pow wow tradition

By Millie Ketcheshawno and John Curl

Celebrate this new annual holiday with us in honor of all of our
ancestors, the people continuing the struggle today and future
generations.

The Grass dancers shake and bend, the high curves of their hair
"roaches" like clipped horses' manes. The men move slowly around
the large chalk circle in the center in the park, stepping to the drum
beat, long ribbons and yarns on their outfits and leggings almost
brushing the ground, the fringes hiding and disguising intricate foot
movements. Beneath a shade outside the circle, a group of Indian
men sit beating time with drum sticks on the large northern drum,
singing in a high falsetto; women join in the chorus.

Hundreds of people on the lawn watch while hundreds of others
mull about the Indian craft and food booths that surround the circle.
Then the drumming suddenly stops and, as if on cue, the dancers all
finish precisely on the last beat.

The men step out of the circle and a group of women dancers
enter, each with an eagle plume atop her head and holding an eagle
wing fan. They are wearing long buckskin and taffeta dresses reaching
down to their ankles, some adorned with metal disks sewn in
patterns. The southern drum group begins a faster tempo. The Jingle-
dress dancers take off with quick movements, disks clattering, a hint
of stiffness in their flowing steps, a sense of calm in their energy.

We are at the Berkeley Indigenous Peoples' Day Pow Wow.

Every year on the Saturday closest to October 12, Berkeley holds
a pow wow and Indian market, to celebrate the survival and
revitalization of Indigenous cultures, and to commemorate Native
resistance to the forces still threatening to destroy them.

What is a Pow wow?

Pow wows offer the most public situation in which non-Indians
are welcome and can connect with Native culture, which is always
around us in mass society but often nearly invisible to those unaware.

There are pow wow dances in which everyone can participate. But although millions of non-Indian people have been to pow wows, many really know little about the meaning of the cultural form or its history.

Many people think that pow wows are a fairly new creation, because until the 1950s most pow wows were very local. It has been said that contemporary pow wows began in the honoring ceremonies for Indian veterans returning after World War II. It was only in the middle of the 1950s that many Indian people began traveling the pow wow highway between Indian communities, dancing while promoting Intertribal culture.

But pow wows go much further back than that. Perhaps the oldest continuous annual one today is the Quapaw pow wow, started over a hundred years ago.

In the early twentieth century a dance known as the Helushka or Hedushka spread out of Oklahoma through the Great Plains north to Canada. Helushka societies were formed in over thirty tribes through the Great Plains region, and through the dance former enemies made peace. The Helushka became the form known today as the Straight Dance; it is the earliest pow wow dance, around which all the others coalesced.

There are different versions of the origin of the Helushka; the historians, as usual, disagree. The Ponca-Omaha are usually credited with the most developed early form. Some say it originated through a vision to a Ponca-Omaha man, and that the earliest Ponca pow wows were celebratory gatherings of the tribe's survival after their forced deportation to Oklahoma from their original homeland in Nebraska. Others historians say the Poncas adapted it from the Pawnee's Irushka ceremony in the middle of the nineteenth century.

Among the Pawnee it was a spiritual dance, taught in a vision to a Pawnee man by a group of beings immersing their hands into boiling water and handling fire. The beings told him they had a new dance to teach him, then held him over the hot coals; after he survived this ordeal, they taught him the songs and dance and told him to take them to the people. Then the beings turned into birds and animals and left. The next night the man climbed a hill to fast; again he met the beings sitting around a fire, singing and laughing. Again he was put to the fire ordeal; again the beings turned into animals and birds. All except one. Then the others left, but the lone being stayed and taught the Pawnee man to make two of the most important symbols of today's male pow wow dancers, the roach headdress and the "crow belt." The roach headdress, made from deer and porcupine hair, represents the fire ordeal. The eagle feather, in a bone spreader made from the shoulder blade of a deer, represents the man standing in the center of fire; the bone represents the medicine given to him. The being taught the man to make many of the other items worn today in the dance, and the first initiate in turn passed them on to his people. The back bustle worn by Fancy dancers is a development from the crow belt.

This vision was acted out in ritual as the dance moved in the early days among the Plains tribes. "Irushka" literally means "they are inside the fire" in the Pawnee language, but is often translated as "warrior." According to this version of history, the Ponca adopted the Pawnee ceremony, but changed the spiritual dance into a commemoration of warriors and war, and therefore also of peacemakers and peace, of cultural resurgence and survival, as tribes who were formerly enemies now danced together. Another version holds that the Ponca had the songs and dances before the Pawnee.

Many tribes also trace pow wows back to their own periodic gatherings, large traditional celebratory feasts, usually after the fall harvest.

The Forms of the Dance

With time and many different tribes adding their individual characters to the dance, the Helushka began to take a variety of forms and different names, such as Grass Dance, Prairie Dance, Wolf Dance and Omaha Dance. At first women did not dance. When non-Indians featured it in nineteenth-century Wild West Shows, as Buffalo Bill did, they called it the "War Dance."

The term pow wow, from the Algonquian word for a gathering of people, began to be used in Oklahoma around 1900.

The Helushka soon took the form on the Southern Plains of the traditional Straight Dance: traditional dancers move proudly and sedately. On the Northern Plains each tribe developed unique styles, such as the Northern Traditional. Over the decades other styles of both male and female dance, movements and songs have developed:

the modern Grass, Fancy and Traditional dances for men; the Shawl, Cloth, Buckskin and Jingle Dances for women. The Shawl Dance is the women's fancy dance, with elaborately beaded or sequined tops and leggings.

The dances continue to develop as more and more tribes outside the Plains tradition have begun to join in pow wows, making social connections with other tribes for friendship, trade and to be part of the Pan-Indian movement.

Pow wows follow a traditional form: they begin with a grand entry, flag ceremony, invocation; followed by a sequence of dances, dance contests, singing, drumming, prayers, speeches, and honoring ceremonies such as giveaways of presents.

There are usually four dance contest categories: tiny tots; boys and girls; young men and women; elder men and women. They compete in Straight/Traditional, Fancy, Grass, Jingle and Shawl Dancing. The contests are judged by people knowledgeable in pow wow style dancing, who may be dancers themselves.

Early pow wows usually held dance contests, but without the cash awards of today.

Pow wows vary from place to place. In some areas a pow wow is primarily a spiritual and traditional celebration, while in other areas it is a more social, secular and commercial event. Many pow wows in Indian Country are not announced in the non-Indian media, and outsiders are rarely invited to some very traditional ceremonies. Indian people from many tribes gather together from every direction to participate in the activities, meet old friends and make new ones, be part of the culture. Almost every week of the year there is at least one pow wow somewhere in the United States and Canada.

Today's Indian Resurgence

Pow wows are integral to today's resurgence of Indian pride, and a primary way that Native people develop inter-tribal culture in a modern context without demanding that each tribe give up its own unique identity. For urban Indians in particular, where Native culture is often very low profile, pow wows are a way of primary public affirmation. pow wows have helped to develop a contemporary context in which each tribal culture can continue, and have helped to

160

create the great movement that is shaping the Indigenous revival of today.

Understanding the modern pow wow is central to recognizing the revitalization of Indigenous culture with its values of respect for the earth, living in traditional balance, respect for the multitude of cultures and creatures on Turtle Island. It is through living our lives in this recognition that we offer hope to move beyond the destructive powers of mass industrial civilization.

•

APPENDIX C

The Indian Market
By Hallie Frazer, Vendor Booth Coordinator

I joined the Committee in 1992, quickly taking on the role of Vendor Booth Coordinator, mentored by Millie Ketcheshawno. I was in awe of the Committee and of how it had come into existence following John Curl's participation in the 1990 "Encuentro" of North and South American Indian leaders held in Ecuador. The time had come, in fulfillment of the ancient Inca prophecy, for the People of the Eagle and the People of the Condor to reunite, restoring harmony and health to the world. This, along with doing what we could to correct the misinformation about Columbus, established the core mission of our PowWow. Celebrating in a centrally located park which was already surrounded by a circular pathway, allowed us to place the dancers in the middle and set the Vendors in a circle encasing the event. Many powwows place their vendors in a separate area, but I felt very strongly that as Native peoples celebrating a sacred event, it was important to mark our interconnectivity by being in circle together. And in the bringing together of the peoples of North and South America, this has proven even more essential. In fact, the success of our powwow is vastly affected by the 'organism' that is created as dancers, drummers, vendors and visitors celebrate as one.

I grew up in a predominantly upscale, white community in the shadow of the Hamptons with a Peruvian-born mother and a father from Alabama. With the expectations we had to live up to in every day life at home, and then trying to relate to our peers at school, I constantly felt that I was straddling the fence between cultures, never totally part of one or the other. It was clear to my siblings and myself that we had indigenous blood from Peru, although this is something that the Peruvian side of the family would rarely admit to. I found myself over the years becoming more and more involved in Native American culture, especially once I moved to Berkeley.

I am very careful about the placement of vendor booths, deliberately interspersing North American vendors with South American to balance them as equally as possible. This caused awkward feelings in early years. It took awhile for some of the North American tribal people to accept the South Americans and Mexican tribal people as "American Indian". And along with that, the relationship that the South American Native vendors have to their indigenousness is different. The exploitation and annihilation that is a matter of every day existence in their home countries, preventing them from education and advancement of any kind, is much more pervasive in the very fabric of the culture, to the point where it has become an "accepted" reality. This vastly affects, generally speaking, their relationship to quality of artisanship. It has been my mission over the years to work with vendors that I accept to encourage authenticity and to ban articles mass-produced in foreign countries or in imitation of traditional tribal art. This is something that I feel passionate about and it has been paying off. But it continues to be an uphill battle, especially when many non-Native customers come and want to pay next to nothing for crafts, and if presented with something made in China, will happily buy it in the spirit of 'a memento' to mark a fun event. I find, however, that this is also changing.

What has also made a difference are the devastating environmental challenges that are now facing the world through the destruction of the Amazonian rain forests and the brutal affect this has on the survival of Native cultures there, some who have just recently had to confront the non-Native world in order to fight for survival. These actions have driven home to many in North America the kinship that both continents share. As a result, tribal leaders from North America have initiated prayer ceremonies with Amazonian tribal chiefs to heal the lands, the waters and the people. The solidarity of the Eagle and the Condor is happening.

APPENDIX D

The Condor and Eagle Encounter
Oral History

By John Curl

One day in the spring of 1990 I saw for the first time a little notice about the Encuentro in the SAIIC newsletter. In early May of that year I met with Nilo Cayuqueo, director of the South and Meso-American Indian Information Center (SAIIC), on East 14th Street in Oakland. SAIIC was organizing the Encuentro in the US, together with other Indian organizations in Ecuador and Columbia. The First Continental Meeting of Indigenous Peoples on the 500 Years of Indian Resistance was scheduled for July 17 to 21 in Quito. Nilo was a soft-spoken Mapuche man with a small mustache and gentle eyes.

I'd already been working on a 1992-focused project as a member of the local chapter of Alliance for Cultural Democracy (ACD), a national multi-ethnic cultural organization (founded in 1976) committed to taking part in the counter-quincentennial campaign. Betty Kano was National Coordinator. ACD would later become a member of Resistance 500.

Nilo asked me about ACD's ideas for organizing a Bay Area-wide cultural festival for 1992. I explained that it was still in the early planning stage; we realized that although non-Indian cultural workers could play an important part by putting forth their visions, we understood that Native people would have the leading role in quincentennial projects. We hoped and expected this lead would come in part from the Encuentro.

Nilo and I talked about trying to get the City of Berkeley involved in the 1992 commemoration. San Francisco was already involved, in a reactionary way. Replicas of Columbus's three ships were sailing from Spain, scheduled to stop in numerous ports, and ultimately dock in San Francisco on October 12, 1992, in conjunction with a huge celebration using Italian-American pride as a cover for a celebration of the colonial/imperialist project. Given Berkeley's history of support for progressive causes, maybe it could be a counter-weight.

Nilo said something like, "Let's invite the mayor of Berkeley to come to the Encuentro."

"It's not very likely that she'd come."

"Then if she can't make it, let's ask her to send a representative," Nilo said.

Several weeks later I was on my way to the airport, as Mayor Loni Hancock's representative to the First Continental Encuentro.

Loni, as I knew her at that time, had deep populist instincts and cared about social justice. When an issue came to the fore, her instinct was usually to use the mayor's office as a catalyst through which the people involved could find their own solutions. I knew Loni pretty well from working in Berkeley Citizens Action (BCA), a local "progressive" political coalition. I was on the BCA steering committee and the editor of their newsletter, as well as a regular worker on Loni's election campaigns. Her first election had been so close there was a recount, and I'd been one of the watchers during the vote recount in the basement of city hall. Later I worked closely with her and community groups for several years to rezone the Berkeley industrial zone to give protections to industries and arts and crafts against runaway gentrifying development, and the city codified those zoning protections in the West Berkeley Plan.

Nilo and I wrote Mayor Hancock a letter which I handed to her. She grasped the situation immediately and came on board. Loni and I then drafted her letter to the Encuentro.

My first contact with the truth about Columbus took place a decade earlier, around 1980, when I was doing some construction work for a homeowner in Oakland. She offered me a box of old magazines. On top of the stack was a beautiful Kuna Indian woman with a gold ring in her nose, the cover of the November, 1975 issue of National Geographic. I opened it to a photo of a hawk with a small bell tied to its foot, in an article about Columbus's voyages in the Caribbean. The photo caption read, in part, "His greed awakened, Columbus demanded of each adult an annual tribute: enough gold dust to fill four hawkbells. Pay or perish. Many Indians fled, but the Spaniards tracked them down with dogs. Thousands ended their lives with poison. In 1492 an estimated 300,000 Indians lived on

Hispaniola. By 1496 a third of them were dead. Less than a decade later the first black slaves arrived to take over the Indians' oppressive burdens."[18]

"I gave them a thousand nice things," wrote Columbus, and the Indians gave him their gold. Among Columbus's presents were hawkbells, possibly including this one (above), found in the area of Navidad. Tied to falcons' legs (top), such bells revealed the locations of straying birds.

His greed awakened, Columbus demanded of each adult an annual tribute: enough gold dust to fill four hawkbells. Pay or perish. Many Indians fled, but the Spaniards tracked them down with dogs. Thousands ended their lives with poison. In 1492 an estimated 300,000 aborigines lived on Hispaniola. By 1496 a third of them were dead. Less than a decade later the first black slaves arrived to take over the Indians' oppressive burdens.

[*National Geographic*, Nov. 1975]

The article actually said very little more about the vicious side of Columbus's history and concentrated on his travels. I later found that to be a pattern in most of the voluminous Columbus literature up until that time: relegated to footnote status in the heroic saga of a great explorer, was his leading the invasion of the Americas, the genocide of the Native peoples, and the founding of the transatlantic slave trade, all perpetrated with full intent by the man we call Columbus.

I continued researching the history, and came to understand how mainstream American culture had painted over the true history and had replaced it with a series of prettified lies and myths. The truth was apparently too disturbing for many people to face, but the lies continued to eat at the heart of our society like a cancer, making us even sicker than the painful truth.

•

Having grown up in New York City, I didn't really get to know Native people until in 1970 I had a job as a social worker on the To'Hajileeji Navajo (Diné) reservation west of Albuquerque, New Mexico. Since the older women spoke little or no English, Alice Werito, a Diné woman who lived on the rez, drove around with me in the all-wheel drive, and acted as interpreter. As we drove through the desert, she taught me a little of the Diné language, and as I became able to say a few thoughts in Diné bizaad, I started to understand Native people a little better. Two of my more memorable moments there involved getting Bernalillo County to pay for a Yeibichai ceremony for a sick boy, and getting a Diné baby girl returned safely home from an Anglo couple who had been foster parenting her. Then I became a woodworker and moved to Berkeley in 1971.

Soon after I first became aware of Columbus's role in the early history of the European invasion of the Americas, I realized that it was almost 500 years since 1492 and, given people's penchant for celebrating the anniversary of almost anything, this was going to be a big one.

•

167

From the plane window the lights of Quito sparkled crisply in the dark mountain air.

Just the day before on a Bay Area Spanish language radio station, I learned that a nationwide general strike was in progress in Ecuador. The English language news made no mention of it. All day I listened carefully to the Spanish news. My understanding of Spanish, like my speaking fluency, was broken and fragmented, but I picked up the gist. The general strike, called by the Ecuadorian labor federation known as FUT (United Workers' Front) was a protest against the government's neoliberal economic policies. Many businesses, factories, public offices, schools, utilities, and transportation facilities were shut down around the country, with some cities entirely paralyzed. But the strike was scheduled for only one day, as a show of force. All was expected to be back to normal by the time I arrived. It was July 13, 1990.

A couple of months previously I only vaguely knew that Ecuador is on the northwest shoulder of South America, below Columbia and above Peru, on the equator. A quick look at a map had told me that the Andes cut like a saw blade through Ecuador's heart, separating the Pacific coastal plain from the Amazon basin. According to my tour book, the Galapagos Islands, 1,000 kilometers out to sea, with their unique wildlife, were the country's main tourist attraction. Ecuador had one of the most ethnically Indian populations on the continent with about 40% of its nine million people traditional indigenous, another 40% mixed, about 10% "white", and the other 10% split between black and Asian. Ten different Indian languages were spoken, the most widespread being Quichua, the Ecuadorian version of Runasimi ("people's language"), the lingua franca of the Andes under the Incas.

The Incas had dominated the Ecuadorean highlands for less than 100 years when the Spaniards arrived. Before that, indigenous civilizations known as Quitus and Caras flourished in the north, Puruhás and Cañarí in the south. Around the year 1450, the Inca army of Tupac Yupanqui, the tenth Sapa Inca (or "emperor") of Tawantinsuyu (or Peru) marched north from Cuzco into Ecuador. Quito fell to the Incas in 1472.

According to my travel book, while periodic civil wars were a constant in much of the Andes, Ecuador had remained comparatively stable in recent times.

Almost as soon as I stepped off the plane I could taste the thin atmosphere, 9,350 feet above sea level. I tired quickly carrying my bags. I slipped into a cab. The only traces of the general strike were slogans painted on numerous walls. As to its significance, the taxi driver shrugged. "We have one or two general strikes in Ecuador every year. The *Levantamiento* last month, the Indian Uprising, now that was something unusual, something which never happened before in my lifetime."

"The what?" I asked.

"Didn't they report it in North America?"

"I must have missed it."

"But nothing will come of it. Nothing ever does."

At the hotel I discovered that I was one of the first participants to arrive. It was four days early. I'd wanted some extra time to poke around as a traveler.

I picked up a local paper. On the front page was an article about CONAIE, the Confederation of Indigenous Nationalities of Ecuador, sponsoring the Encuentro. But the Encuentro was not mentioned. The article talked about the Indian Uprising, how negotiations with the government had broken down, the main points of contention being the Agrarian Reform Law and the creation of a fund that would enable Indigenous communities to purchase their own traditional lands.

The next day I went down to the CONAIE building, a large structure that they had obtained by squatting several years previously, at the corner of Avenida Los Granados and Avenida 6 de Diciembre. The lobby was bustling with activity. On the floor several people were painting a huge canvas. In the center was the sun and the crescent moon joined together, circled by a rainbow. On one side was the face of an Indian man, a condor emerging from his forehead; on the other side was the face of an Indian woman, an eagle emerging from her forehead. The wing tips of the two great birds met in a circle. The painter, Lligalo Abel, looked up at me. "Do you like it?"

"It's very powerful. What does it mean?"

"This is the symbol of the Encuentro. The Condor and the Eagle. It's based on a old story, a prophesy of the Andes."

[Photos by John Curl]

The CONAIE Building in Quito

I introduced myself at the office. A young woman named Monica rummaged through a file, pulled out the copy of the Berkeley mayor's statement that I had sent down, and asked me to write a translation. I fumbled with the task for a while, then noticed a stack of new books on the table, "The Indigenous Uprising in the Ecuadorian Press," published by CONAIE. I picked one up. Most of it was a compilation of recent press clippings. I slowly pieced together the events of the previous weeks.

Beginning on June 4, the Indians of Ecuador seized land that had traditionally belonged to their communities. In the Indigenous tradition, individuals do not own land; the community owns the land and assigns it to individuals to use. But since the Spanish conquest, great haciendas claimed almost all the land, while most Native people were made landless. In 1965 a progressive military junta decreed the Agrarian Reform Law. Any land left fallow for two years could be bought by a landless person to farm, in order to put all farmable land to use. A new constitution guaranteed "to the producer the right to hold land."

But the hacienderos found ways to stall out the Agrarian Reform Law, and for 25 years it was scarcely implemented. So on June 4, 1990, the Indians went into motion. They moved onto parts of forty haciendas left fallow for two years. They demanded that the government resolve 70 long-standing land disputes and pay 90% of the cost of the lands. They blocked major roads all over Ecuador with rocks and logs. They held huge marches and rallies, with a half million people in the streets. They seized churches in Quito and Guayaquil. They demanded that the government stop foreign oil companies from destroying the Amazon, and order them out of the country. The Uprising was timed as a protest against upcoming local elections, in which everyone was required to vote but which were rigged and never changed anything. Casualties of the Levantamiento: many injured, one dead.

•

LEVANTAMIENTO INDÍGENA

A los 500 años de la invasión europea, los pueblos indígenas del Continente, nos hemos unido firmemente para luchar por la supresión de todas las formas de opresión neocolonialista.

Tradicionalmente los estados nacionales se han negado a reconocer nuestros legítimos derechos como pueblos diversos, porque somos portadores de una historia, culturas, idiomas y tradiciones que hemos defendido durante 500 años.

Creemos que Nuestra América, Nuestra Pacha Mama, Nuestra Abya Yala puede ser una sola fuerza unida por el reconocimiento de la existencia de los distintos pueblos y el respeto y garantía para nuestro desarrollo político, social, económico y cultural. Estamos convencidos que esta aspiración nuestra debe ser compartida y apoyada por todos los sectores sociales conscientes de la necesidad de la emancipación definitiva de nuestros países.

14

Esta lucha ha sido permanente en estos 500 años y hoy el Levantamiento Indígena del Ecuador, de los días 4, 5 y 6 de junio de 1990 es una muestra de que nuestro proceso avanza. Este levantamiento es ya un hecho Histórico por que tuvo la fuerza de la unidad, una organización nacional nace de nuestras propias aspiraciones y recoge nuestras tradicionales formas de lucha, heredadas de Rumiñahui, Túpac Amaru, Túpac Katari, Daquilema.

Este levantamiento debe obligar a reflexionar y replantear a los Gobiernos y a todas las sociedades sobre las tradicionales formas de opresión y explotación a las que hemos estado sometidos.

El levantamiento fue la expresión de nuestra dignidad, nadie puede negar su autenticidad, su fuerza y la unidad indígena que demostró.

No podemos dejar de reconocer y agradecer la solidaridad recibida por importantes sectores del país, quienes cumplieron papel fundamental al reconocer y comprender la validez de nuestros planteamientos. Por otro lado, condenamos la violencia desatada en contra de nuestras comunidades y organizaciones por parte del Gobierno y sectores de terratenientes.

La CONAIE vio en el diálogo con el Gobierno el espacio para llegar a las soluciones concretas y urgentes de las reivindicaciones inmediatas planteadas por las organizaciones; sin embargo, el Gobierno no ha demostrado la voluntad política para responder nuestras peticiones y el diálogo se ha roto. Las acciones que se desaten como consecuencia de este rompimiento serán de absoluta responsabilidad del Gobierno.

Los indios amamos la paz, pero estamos dispuestos a defender con dignidad nuestros derechos.

"1992 NI UNA HACIENDA EN EL ECUADOR"

shunk shunkulla	shunk shimilla
shunk yuyailla	Runa Kaspaka
shunk makilla	Kuna Kanchik

15

Nearing the 500 years of the European invasion, the Indigenous peoples of this continent have firmly united to struggle to suppress all forms of neo-colonialist oppression.

Traditionally, the national states have refused to recognize our legitimate rights as a diverse people, in spite of the fact that we have been the carriers of history, culture, language and traditions that we have defended during these 500 years.

We believe that Our America, Pacha Mama (the Earth), Our Abya Yala, can be a single, united force working for the recognition of the existence of distinct peoples and the respect and guarantee for our political, social, economic and cultural development.

This has been a never ending struggle during these 500 years; and today, the Indian Uprising of Ecuador, from the 4th, 5th, and 6th of June, 1990 is a demonstration that this process is advancing. This uprising is already a historical fact because it had the strength of

172

unity. The uprising is where a national organization has been born of our own aspirations and it takes up our traditional forms of struggle, inherited from Rumiñahui, Tupac Amaru, Tupac Katari, and Daquilema. This uprising should oblige the governments and all of the societies to reflect and rethink their traditional forms of oppression and exploitation to which we have been submitted.

This uprising was the expression our dignity and no one can negate or deny its authenticity, its strength and the unity of Indian people that it demonstrated.

We cannot forget to recognize and appreciate the solidarity we received from important sectors of this country, all of whom have played a fundamental role in recognizing and comprehending the validity of our proposals. On the other hand, we condemn the violence unleashed against our communities and organizations by the government and sectors of the landowners.

CONAIE saw in the dialogue with the government the space to arrive at concrete and urgent solutions to immediate vindication of the resolutions proposed by the organizations; nevertheless, the government has not demonstrated the political will to respond to our petitions and the dialogue has been broken. The actions unleashed as a consequence of this rupture will be the absolute responsibility of the government.

The Indian people love peace but we are disposed to defend our rights with dignity.

"Not One Hacienda in Ecuador in 1992"

hunk shunkulla	one heart
shunk yuyailla	one thought
shunk makilla	one hand
shunk shimilla	one mouth
RunaKaspaka	The People's Path
Kuna Kanchik	Now in Light

•

After I left the CONAIE building, I went off alone to the Quito zoo. It was almost empty, perhaps because of the late hour, perhaps because of its strange location inside a military academy: the cadets were the zoo keepers. I sat in front of an outdoor cage and watched four huge condors perched on a rocky crag, dark gray bodies with white necks and wings, bald purplish heads, the male with a comb on top. One condor spread its massive wings, swooped down to the ground, picked up a piece of flesh, then flew back again. I found four small feathers on the grass nearby.

Back at the hotel desk was a note to me from two SAIIC people, Peter Veilleux and Elizabeth Bobsy Draper, to come down to see them in another room. The tiny room was filled with boxes; literature being prepared for the Encuentro was spread out on the cramped beds. But for no apparent reason (all the conference-reserved rooms were the same price), the hotel had given me a large two-room suite. The Encuentro office moved into my living room.

But Nilo Cayuqueo, the director of SAIIC, a Mapuche, and his close associate Wara Alderete, a Calchaqui, hadn't arrived. Finally word came that they'd been detained by the police in Argentina, where they'd stopped off. We'd have to proceed without them.

I soon had several roommates, including Ed Burnstick.

The English-speaking and the Spanish-speaking delegates were lodged in separate hotels, which seemed strange to me, although it did simplify the language problem. Ed said that it reflected past difficulties. He was a veteran of international Indigenous conferences, including the 1977 UN Geveva conference, and had seen many communication breakdowns between Latin American and North American Indians. He explained that the historical experiences of Indians in the Latin and Anglo colonial worlds were different in many ways, creating problems of cultural understanding. While North American Indian history is filled with hundreds of broken treaties by England and later the US, Spain never made any treaties and never recognized any sovereign Indian nations. The Spaniards conquered and enslaved, while the Anglos primarily wanted the land and removed the Native peoples by any means. I noticed on the list of Indian organizations invited to the Encuentro, none of the organizations were from the US or Canada. All the Northern participants had come as individuals through SAIIC, and not as official delegates of their organizations.

Although at this time I did not know anything about the 1977 UN International Non-Governmental Organizations' Conference on Indigenous Peoples of the Americas in Geneva, problematic dynamics between North-South there reflected that same friction, although other factors were also involved.

Ed Burnstick was a large, gentle Cree-Nakoda elder from Canada, a traditional person from a reserve in Alberta, where as a youth he lived the hunting and trapping ways of his people. He'd been a hoop dancer, and worked in construction and logging. He was also somewhat tech savvy, and helped develop one of the first native run radio stations in Canada. As an activist, he had been instrumental in the first grouping of the American Indian Movement (AIM) in Canada, and the International Indian Treaty Council (IITC). He served a term as chief of his tribe, Paul First Nation band of Woodlands Crees, and later as interim president of the Confederacy of Treaty Six First Nations. He'd been a delegate at the United Nations conference in Geneva in 1977, where the Native delegations issued the very first call to replace Columbus Day with Indigenous Peoples Day.

But all I knew about him at that time, in 1990, was that Ed Burnstick was strong, kind, humble, and wise. Ed deepened my understanding of the problems and helped direct me toward solutions.

Ed explained to me about Indigenous peoples, the ones who never set out to conquer the world, but stayed in their communities, cared for their land in sustainable ways, and tried to live in peace and harmony with their neighbors. For Ed, the key to life had already been passed down to us by our ancestors: the most important thing is right living, which is only possible by following true ways as part of a community. Indigenous peoples are the custodians not only of their own communities and the future generations, but of a living philosophy of respect and caring for the natural world, of Mother Earth, so the struggle for Native rights and community common land is also the struggle to protect the global environment and ensure the survival of all peoples and the planet. Indigenous people were bringing this message to the world today, according to Ed Burnstick, possibly the most important message the world needed to learn, as we teetered on the brink of self-destruction. The entire colonial enterprise, based on the genocide of the Indigenous peoples, needed to be reversed.

That was the first time I had ever heard anyone speak of the world as being divided between Indigenous people and nonIndigenous people, and it took me a while to wrap my head around the concept.

•

After the opening session in Quito, we took off on busses for the conference center, Campamento La Merced, about an hour and a half into the Andes mountains. We arrived at dusk. Word circulated that the surrounding hills were crawling with police.

We were encircled by mountain peaks. Scattered about were a variety of meeting rooms and facilities. In the center was a large circus-sized tent, with many rows of benches. Nearby was a lake with a few rowboats.

I was assigned to a small cabin with eight other men, all Indian, about half from the Pacific Northwest and Canada. Besides Ed Burnstick were Ray Williams (Swinomish), Mark Kremen (Yakama), and Eugene Hazgood, (Diné). I grabbed a lower in a triple-decker bunk bed. Dan, a Chicano from southern Texas, quickly found the showers in a building about halfway to the dining hall. I assumed they were going to be crowded that night, so I decided to wait and get up very early.

I woke at 5 a.m. and staggered in the dark toward the bath building. Halfway there I met a man from my room, Tom, coming back. He told me that in the middle of his shower the lights and water suddenly went out. I fumbled my way over and watched the sad dripping faucets for myself.

Someone mentioned that they were starting the sacred fire, so I headed down to the lake. Ed Burnstick was there, Rose Auger, her son Michael, and a group of others. Ed, it turned out, was one of the spiritual leaders. They lit a kindling of grasses, nurtured a small flame with twigs and sticks until it grew into a dancing blaze. Four men were honored to be firekeepers, with two alternates; they would make sure that the flames stayed healthy until the end of the Encuentro. One of the firekeepers, I believe, was Tupac Enrique Acosta. Dawn ceremonies were scheduled every morning at 6 a.m. by the fire.

15 Dias, 26 Julio, 1990

I sat on my towel near the fire; the ground was damp and there was no room on the grass mats. In the sky I could see the constellation the Southern Cross. The women sat to the north of the fire, the men to the south. Ed announced that Rose, the primary spiritual leader, had received permission to break with tradition and briefly permit photographs during the pipe ceremony. The purpose of this was to show the reporters, who were there in force, that we had nothing to hide. Many people were unhappy with this decision but we continued.

177

[*Unity*, 8/31/1990]

Nilo Cayuqueo and Rose Auger

Smoldering sage was brought to each person; the smoke purified and blessed each face and head. The pipe was filled with ceremonial tobacco, lit with grass braids. Each took a drag, turned it once clockwise and passed it to the next in the circle. This was the first time in over twenty years that I'd smoked tobacco, the first time ever ceremonially, and it made me very high. Rose handed lengths of colored cloth, symbolizing the four directions, to different people, who circled the fire, then placed the cloths as offerings into the flames. A thin crescent moon, cupped upward, rose between two peaks, followed by a glorious sunrise.

Before we dispersed, a man in Andean clothes announced that the following morning at 5 a.m., even before the North American sunrise ceremonies, traditional Incan dawn ceremonies would be held.

According to Ed Burnstick, there was no equivalent in the US or Canada of the Ecuadorian national confederation CONAIE or the Columbian ONIC. The Latin American Indian people were more represented by large organizations than the Northern Nations. Ed said that many North American Indians were quite frustrated with their tribal governments and organizations, and considered many of them to be fabrications by the dominant society, and not representative of traditional ways.

15Dias, 26 Jullio, 1990

[*Hoy*, 22 Julio, 1990]

Líderes campesinos de varios países asisten en Quito al primer encuentro continental de pueblos indígenas. Discutirán problemas comunes y presentarán manifestaciones de su rica y milenaria cultura.

[*El Comercio*, 17 Julio, 1990]

Nilo Cayuqueo (Mapuche, Argentina and Oakland, California, South and Meso-American Indian Information Center coordinator) speaking at the sunrise ceremony in Quito.

[Photo by Bobsy Draper, *Crossroads*, Oct. 1990, No. 3]
Sunrise Ceremony at the Encuentro

At the last minute Nilo Cayuqueo, the SAIIC director, and Wara Alderete arrived. They had been harassed by authorities in Argentina, but finally managed to get to Peru and cross by land into Ecuador.

But almost simultaneously word came that a delegate from Columbia had been arrested at the border for carrying a few coca leaves, traditional among his people. Unknown men falsely identifying themselves as CONAIE had appeared at the other hotel and taken the names and passport numbers of all the Latino delegates. At the airport arriving North American Indians had been photographed. Security measures had to be taken.

The next morning was registration then a press conference. Frantic preparations of the packets continued most of the night. I overheard Agnes say that she went to the zoo to get a condor feather, but the guard told her it was closed and didn't let her pass. I gave her one of mine.

At breakfast I heard that government harassment was suspected in the mysterious power outage and a delegation had gone to the Ministry of the Interior to complain.

We gathered in the big tent.

The gathering began with a discussion of who could vote on resolutions. Delegates had different statuses: official, fraternal and observer. Each Indian nation, tribe or organization could have only one "official" delegate, the others being "fraternal". Non-Indians were almost entirely "observers", with a couple of "fraternal" exceptions including myself. However, on the workshop resolutions each country needed to choose only one voting member, to prevent domination by the large and well-represented countries. The North Americans were not too happy with this, and thought it made more sense for each Indian nation and tribe to have a vote. We were briefly stuck on the organizational differences between north and south. The south prevailed. Each country caucused, and the US delegation chose Laurie Weahkee, a young Cochiti-Diné-Zuni woman from New Mexico as the voting official.

Everyone needed to choose one of eight simultaneous workshops to discuss different issue-areas for the next two days. Each workshop had literature to aid discussion. The topics were: the position of indigenous peoples on the 500th anniversary; Indian self-determination and political activity; education, culture and religion; indigenous organizing; women; land and natural resources; indigenous legislation; human rights and political prisoners. I chose to go to the 500th anniversary workshop.

Our workshop worked on a long list of resolutions and observations to be sorted out, refined, boiled down, and brought before the entire conference, along with the resolutions from all the other commissions, on the last day.

Only hours after the sunrise ceremony, word circulated that the morning Quito newspaper had a front page photo of the pipe ceremony with a caption saying that "pagan rituals" were being held, implying some kind of defilement. Many traditional people were unhappy that photos had been permitted; some proposed extinguishing the fire. But the decision was made to continue.

Suddenly the electricity and water came back on, and there was a rush for the showers.

At lunch I talked with Rafael Pandam, vice-president of CONAIE and his friend Jesús, two men with long straight hair and bangs, from an area in the Amazon jungle near the town of Puyo, down the sheer eastern slope of the Andes, by the headwaters of the world's greatest river. They explained that the entire Ecuadorian Amazon has been signed over as "concessions" to oil companies. These were destroying both the natural environment and the indigenous people who have lived in relatively untouched isolation until recently. They invited me to come down to Puyo after the conference, to provide me with documentation so I could let the outside world know what was happening there.

I had already planned to fly to the city of Cuenca in the southern highlands after the conference, and then return north slowly by bus, to see the entire country. Rafael told me I could easily turn east at the halfway point and detour down to the Amazon for a couple of days.

My next morning began again in the dark by the fire. The Andean spiritual leader explained that he would lead the group in ancient dawn ceremonies that in Inca times were performed every morning, but which had been banned by the early Spaniards. They had been preserved by a small number of people. He asked everyone to face east and quietly prayed while burning coca leaves. Then sitting on his heels, he spread his arms and brought his head slowly to the ground, imploring Pacha Mama (the Earth) and Inti (the Sun). The group followed him in unison many times. Then he stretched his feet back and continued with a kind of push-up, which most people followed. It was very reminiscent of yoga dawn exercises. Tomorrow, he said, everyone should bring some unnatural article from the dominant civilization, which we would burn symbolically.

Finally the moon appeared, as it did the previous morning, followed quickly by dawn. As the light spread, Rose and Ed took over and passed the ceremonial pipes. Several Guatemalan women in huipiles walked on their knees around the fire. Rose gave a pinch of the ceremonial tobacco to everyone. "Keep it in a special place." At the end of the conference, when the fire was extinguished, they would distribute the ashes.

A controversy arose between the political and spiritual leaders. Rose said that for spiritual reasons it was very important that the Encuentro end here around the sacred fire, and not disperse back to the National Congress in Quito as planned. She said that the Encuentro would be over when the fire was extinguished. The political leaders said they must return to Quito. There was a deadlock.

We returned back to the final workshop sessions, then in the afternoon to a marathon plenary, bringing all the resolutions for full discussion. This lasted well into the night.

The nonIndian statement of solidarity began, "we stand with you to achieve a fundamental restructuring of the social and economic order..."

During the report from the Indigenous Women's commission, came a sudden uproar. The delegate from Nicaragua, several days late, had finally arrived, and the proceedings were interrupted for him to speak.

The political-spiritual controversy was resolved. Rose Auger would deliver a prayer at the final plenary in Quito, then return to conference grounds in the mountain to extinguish the ceremonial fire.

The next morning at 5 a.m., Saturday, July 21st, the last fire dawn ceremony began. The Inca exercise-prayers were repeated, followed by the symbolic burning, in a separate fire, of unnatural objects such as a soda can, a plastic fork, styrofoam packing. Then Rose and Ed brought out several pipes for the final ceremony. Certain people were honored for their extraordinary contributions, and testified before the fire. The firekeepers received a special blessing. Rose asked if anyone had questions. The Latin Americans had many. They seemed to recognize that the North American ceremonies were very close to the cultural sources that they were seeking to return to, without the overlay of Catholicism that permeated many Indian ceremonies of Latin America.

[Photo by John Curl]

The final colored cloth offerings were placed on the fire, and as they burned, I searched the sky for the moon, but it was nowhere to be seen. The sun broke brilliantly over the mountain. I realized that dawn on the last day had brought the fulfillment of the symbol of the Encuentro: the sun and moon were in conjunction; the sun had swallowed the moon.

I packed hurriedly; the busses were waiting. As I left my room, an Ecuadorian Indian man in a red poncho, Manuel de la Cruz, pulled me aside. His community was on the lower slopes of the great snow-capped volcano Cotapaxi, about 100 miles away. His countryside was being devastated. Much of the Ecuadorian highlands, he explained, had been deforested. A national reforestation program, active in recent decades, had used foreign trees, eucalyptus and oregon pine, which grow rapidly, but their leaves and needles contain substances which ruin the earth so no crops will grow. He asked me if I know any North American organization that might help in replacing these destructive trees with native Ecuadorian ones.

I thought of Eric from the organization Arctic to Amazon Alliance. But he was nowhere around. I assured Manuel that I would try to find him before the day ended.

At the bus I was talking to Marie-Helene Laraque of Haiti (and Canada), who had also attended the 1977 UN Geneva conference, when I noticed that her name tag said Taino. I was stunned, as I thought that Columbus's genocide of the Taino people of Caribbean had been complete and total. She explained that even in genocide there are survivors. We boarded the busses and headed down toward Quito.

It hadn't hit me until now, but almost all the trees along the road were eucalyptus. I knew them so well from their domination and sterilization of much of the California hills in Berkeley and Oakland, where a century ago they replaced a redwood forest that once grew so tall it was a landmark for ships entering the Golden Gate.

Inside the National Congress filled up.

Just as I sat down, Adela Principe Diego, in a traditional Peruvian dress, came over to me, accompanied by Bobsy Draper. Adela had just been stopped at the entrance by an official from her embassy: "We hear you've been saying bad things about Peru. You will come to the embassy to talk about this." Adela said that in her country many people and their families are "disappeared" for less cause than this. She asked if I would be part of a group she was organizing to go with her. I assured her I would.

15 Dias, 26 Julio, 1990

Speeches were made, to a constant flash of bulbs. Rose took the podium and weaved in a spiritual context. Musicians brought down the house. The Declaration of Quito was read and passed around. As the president of CONAIE announced the Encuentro at an end, I signed the Declaration.

[*Huracán* Vo. 1 No. 1, Fall/Winter 1990]
Maria Toj at the Press Conference

Then back on the busses for festivities at Huaycopungo, a town in the mountains near the weaving center of Ota Valo.

I was in the lead bus, flying the rainbow CONAIE flag, the ancient banner of the Incas, on a pole taped to the sideview mirror. At first the land was barren, desertlike, with occasional stands of eucalyptus. Then as we got higher, it became greener, and we were in farm country. To my disappointment I saw no llamas, only typical barnyard animals. Someone said that llamas were not used here any more but were still common in Peru.

We stopped by a gravel road, where a crowd with banners and signs welcomed us. "Is this Huaycopungo, where the fiesta is?" I asked someone. "No, this is Pijal, this is different, you'll see." We walked down the road, teetered on logs across a swampy stretch, across a meadow. A stallion with wild eyes ran toward us; the crowd broke to let him through. We crossed a recently-plowed field to a small settlement where about two hundred children, women and men were gathered.

We formed a wide circle around a volleyball court; a woman stepped forward and explained:

"This land has always belonged to the community of Pijal, as far back as anyone knows. But this land was stolen by the rich *hacienderos*, and the people have suffered hardships for generations. Now in the great Indigenous Uprising we the people of Pijal have taken back our land and have begun to farm it and we will never let it be stolen from us again."

In her simple statement, in the determined expressions on the faces around me, I saw a people who had passed beyond hopelessness and rediscovered hope.

Then on to Fiesta Huaycopungo. We lined up and received our dinner of corn, salsa and beef in a small brown paper bag. Sitting on an empty lot near several pigs, in the distance I saw Lake San Pablo. Everyone drifted down to a field near the town's center, where the entire population was gathering.

I noticed Eric and asked him about reforestation. He said that is exactly the kind of project his organization does. I glanced around, picked out the red poncho of Manuel, and brought them together.

Word arrived that two others had been called before their embassies, a Guatemalan and a Nicaraguan, both women.

As darkness set in, the horizon began to flash with heat lightning. A group of four horsemen suddenly appeared, bearing red flags, followed by masked and costumed men on foot, one with a dog face, one in a sack and carrying a chicken, one with a wheel on top of a pole, oranges and bananas tied to it. Another horseman followed, wearing a mask with strings of colored beads hanging down his face, shaded by a black umbrella. They rode once around the field, then into the center, where those on foot danced in a circle. I asked a nearby man for an explanation. He said the horsemen with the red pennants appear at the planting time fiesta, and the bead-faced man, named Corasas, appears every year after the harvest.

Then music and dancing began in earnest, one band after the other. All joined hands and danced in long chains which kept changing direction. Men carrying soda bottles full of firewater called *trago* plied everyone with toasts. Then traditional and choreographed dance groups came on one after another.

A man pulled me aside, introduced himself as a reporter from a newspaper in Spain, asked if he could interview me, and wanted to know why I was here. I tried to tell him but could hardly find the words in Spanish. He said, "Don't you think it's patronizing for a North American to come down here and be part of this?"

Before I could answer, three Ecuadorian Indian men offered us a toast. The reporter asked one of them, "Wouldn't you like to be rich?"

The man responded, "Sure."

The Spaniard turned back to me and said, "See, all this stuff about communal land, when in reality they're just capitalists like everybody else."

I realized that the reporter had come here with the mission of returning with a story that he couldn't find here. There was a touch of desperation on his face.

The busses were leaving back to Quito. The fiesta would continue all night. Those who stayed were welcome to sleep on mats

191

in the communal hall. At the last minute I felt very tired, and decided to return to Quito.

At the hotel I met some old friends: Rupert from the Maroon colony in Jamaica; Irvince, from the island of Dominica; Cindi Alvitre, a California Gabrieleña; Ed, Rose, Paul Haible, Nilok Butler, Eugene Hasgood from Big Mountain, so many more.

Also in the hotel hall I got into a conversation with a young woman. At first I thought she had been at the Encuentro, but then she told me no. She was part of a group of four Columbians who recently had to flee their country because they had been working for social change. In a couple of months their Ecuadorian visas would expire and they would be expelled. If they were forced to return to Columbia, they would probably be killed. They were looking for a third country to escape to. Did I know of any human rights organization that might help them?

The next day, Monday, July 23, I was scheduled to go to the Peruvian embassy with Adela and a group of others. Then on Tuesday I was due to fly south. But it turned out that Monday was a national holiday, Simon Bolívar's birthday. I agonized over it, then decided that enough people would be going to the embassy without me.

I flew down to the southern highlands, walked around Cuenca a bit, then hit the road. An incredible two days by bus through the mountains. I traveled by pickup truck to Inga Pirca, the only complete Inca ruins in Ecuador, with an oval sun temple.

Then down, straight down, to the Amazon, following the Río Pastaza, along hairpin turns, great precipices, rope bridges, waterfalls everywhere, one cascading over the top of the bus, washed-out roads, jungle vegetation, a bad tire, a crate of chicks peeping all the way. The bus stopped at the military base in the town called Shell, once the oil center of the country. They checked my passport. What are you doing here? Tourist. Not far away was the border, and beyond that a huge area that Peru reportedly stole in a war in 1941 (while most of the world was focused on World War 2), and that Ecuador still disputed. Relations between the two countries were still not the best.

I finally arrived in Puyo and took a taxi into the jungle to the office of CONFENAIE, one of the Indian organizations making up CONAIE.

As bad luck would have it, my friends Rafael and Jesús were not there, but would be back Friday, too late for me. At first I was crestfallen, but then talked to the secretary, Luisa, and she took me into the office to speak with Luis Vargas, the president of CONFENAIE, who had been at the Encuentro. Luis and Luisa showed me a map of the area. The entire Amazon was cut up among Texaco, Conoco, Tenneco, ESSO, BP and other companies. Shell Oil, the original perpetrator, decided that better profits were elsewhere, and was long gone.

The destruction by the oil and logging companies was mostly visible from the air, they explained. Just as in our country, the corporations left "view corridors" around highways so drivers could remain unaware of the devastation behind the thin wall of trees. It was so bad, they told me, that if it continued at the current rate, much of the Ecuadorian Amazon could be a desert in twenty years.

Back on the bus, creeping up the mountain passes. We stopped at a narrow turn; the driver's helper got out, looked up and motioned ambiguously. The driver cautiously began again. But most of the people in the bus shouted No! and he stopped. The man next to me said, "Landslide." Rocks were tumbling down from the hill about thirty feet in front of us. We got out to watch. A few rocks at a time fell for about ten minutes, then suddenly a large chunk of hill came loose, and six foot boulders hurdled down, completely blocking the road. A half hour later bulldozers cleared it and we hurried on.

I spent my last days back north in Ota Valo, the weaving center famous since before the Incas came to Ecuador from Peru in the 1400s. I wandered through their incredible Saturday market. In the central plaza was a statue of Rumiñahui, leader of the Resistance to the Spanish invasion and Indian Ecuador's national hero. It was a time of reflection.

For the Indian peoples, 1992 represented the culmination of 500 years of invasion and occupation. It also represented 500 years of resistance and struggle for self-determination. The former was cause to grieve and the latter cause to celebrate.

The First Continental Conference, the Encuentro, helped to raise the consciousness of American Indigenous peoples to a new level. For the first time they had formed a direct continental network using the latest communications technology, were in constant contact on a hemispheric level, and many were coordinating common struggles for self-determination.

The Encuentro left a legacy to all of us here in the Americas (or Turtle Island, or Abya Yala, as they say in the Andes), and a path forward: the joining of the Condor's and Eagle's tears.

•

APPENDIX E

DECLARATION OF QUITO, 1990

The Continental Gathering "500 Years of Indian Resistance," with representatives from 120 Indian Nations, International and Fraternal organizations, meeting in Quito, July 17-20, 1990, declare before the world the following:

The Indians of America have never abandoned our constant struggle against the conditions of oppression, discrimination and exploitation which were imposed upon us as a result of the European invasion of our ancestral territories.

Our struggle is not a mere conjectural reflection of the memory of 500 years of oppression which the invaders, in complicity with the "democratic" governments of our countries, we want to turn it into events of jubilation and celebration. Our Indian People, Nations and Nationalities are basing our struggle on our identity, which shall lead us to true liberation. We are responding aggressively, and-commit ourselves to reject this "celebration."

The struggle of our People has acquired a new quality in recent times. This struggle is less isolated and more organized. We are now completely conscious that our total liberation can only be expressed through the complete exercise of our self-determination. Our unity is based on this fundamental right. Our self-determination is not just a simple declaration.

We must guarantee the necessary conditions that permit complete exercise of our self-determination; and this, in turn must be expressed as complete autonomy for our Peoples. Without Indian self-government and without control of our territories, there can be no autonomy.

The achievement of this objective is a principal task for Indian Peoples however, through our struggles we have learned that our problems are not different, in many respects, from those of other popular sectors. We are convinced that we must march alongside the peasants, the workers, the marginalized sectors, together with intellectuals committed to our cause, in order to destroy the dominant system of oppression and construct a new society, pluralistic, democratic and humane, in which peace Is guaranteed.

The existing nation states of the Americas, their constitutions and fundamental laws are judicial/political expressions that negate our socio-economic, cultural and political rights.

From this point in our general strategy of struggle, we consider it to be a priority that we demand complete structural change; change which recognizes the inherent right to self-determination through Indian own governments and through the control of our territories.

Our problems will not be resolved through the self-serving politics of governmental entities which seek integration and ethno-development. it is necessary to have an integral transformation at the level of the state and national society; that is to say, the creation of a new nation.

In this Gathering it has been clear that territorial rights are a fundamental demand of the Indigenous Peoples of the Americas.

Based on these aforementioned reflections, the organizations united in the First Continental Gathering of Indigenous Peoples reaffirm:

1. Our emphatic rejection of the Quincentennial celebration, and the firm promise that we will turn that date into an occasion to strengthen our process of continental unity and struggle towards our liberation.

2. Ratify our resolute political project of self-determination and conquest of our autonomy, in the framework of nation states, under a new popular order, respecting the appellation which each People determines for their struggle and project.

3. Affirm our decision to defend our culture, education, and religion as fundamental to our Identity as Peoples, reclaiming and maintaining our own forms of spiritual life and communal coexistence, in an intimate relationship with our Mother Earth.

4. We reject the manipulation of organizations which are linked to the dominant sectors of society and have no Indigenous representation, who usurp our name for (their own) Imperialist

interests. At the same time, we affirm our choice to strengthen our own organizations, without excluding or Isolating ourselves from other popular struggles.

5. We recognize the important role that Indigenous women play in the struggles of our Peoples. We understand the necessity to expand women's participation in our organizations and we reaffirm that it is one struggle, men and women together, in our liberation process, and a key question in our political practices.

6. We Indian Peoples consider it vital to defend and conserve our natural resources, which right now are being attacked by transnational corporations. We are convinced that this defense will be realized if it is Indian People who administer and control the territories where we live, according to our own principles of organization and communal life.

7. We oppose national judicial structures which are the result of the process of colonization and neo-colonization. We seek a New Social Order that embraces our traditional exercise of Common Law, an expression of our culture and forms of organization. We demand that we be recognized as Peoples under International Law, and that this recognition be incorporated into the respective Nation States.

8. We denounce the victimization of Indian People through violence and persecution, which constitutes a flagrant violation of human rights. We demand respect for our right to life, to land, to free organization and expression of our culture. At the same time we demand the release of our leaders who are held as political prisoners, an end to repression, and restitution for the harms caused us.

•

APPENDIX F

THE 1977 GENEVA CONFERENCE
FINAL RESOLUTION

The International Non-Governmental Organizations Conference on Discrimination against Indigenous Populations 1977 in the Americas brought together more than 250 delegates, observers and guests at the Palais des Nations, Geneva, from 20-23 September, including representatives of more than 50 international nongovernmental organizations.

For the first time, the widest and most united representation of indigenous nations and peoples, from the Northern to the most Southern tip and from the far West to the East of the Americas took part in the Conference.

They included representatives of more than 60 Nations and peoples, from fifteen countries (Argentina, Bolivia, Canada, Chile, Costa Rica, Guatemala, Ecuador, Mexico, Nicaragua, Panama Paraguay, Peru, Surinam, United States of America, Venezuela).

It is regretted that some delegates were prevented by their governments from attending.

The Director of the United Nations Division on Human Rights addressed the participants on behalf of the United Nations Secretary-General. Representatives of the United Nations, the International Labour Organization and UNESCO addressed and participated in the conference. The representative of the Consel d'Etat of the Canton of Geneva welcomed the participants. Observers from 38 UN Member States followed the proceedings. The Conference was the fourth such event organized by the Geneva NGO Sub-Committee on Racism, Racial Discrimination, Apartheid and Decolonization of the Special NGO Committee on Human Rights.

Previous conferences, all organized within the framework of the United Nations Decade for Action to Combat Racism and Racial Discrimination were, in 1974, against apartheid and colonialism in Africa; in 1975, on discrimination against migrant workers in Europe; in 1976, on the situation of political prisoners in southern Africa.

The representatives of the indigenous peoples gave evidence to the international community of the ways in which discrimination, genocide and ethnocide operated. While the situation may vary from country to country, the roots are common to all; they include the brutal colonization to open the way for plunder of their land and resources by commercial interests seeking maximum profits; the massacres of millions of native peoples for centuries and the continuous grabbing of their land which deprives them of the possibility of developing their own resources and means of livelihood; the denial of self-determination of indigenous nations and peoples destroying their traditional value system and their social and cultural fabric. The evidence pointed to the continuation of this oppression resulting in the further destruction of the indigenous nations.

Many participants expressed support for and solidarity with the indigenous nations and peoples.

Three commissions dealt specifically with the legal, economic, and social and cultural aspects of discrimination and formulated recommendations for actions in support of indigenous peoples. Based on these reports, the Conference established a program of actions to be carried out by non-governmental organizations in accordance with their mandates and possibilities:

PROGRAMME OF ACTIONS

The Conference recommends:

• to observe October 12, the day of so-called "discovery" of America, as an International Day of Solidarity with the Indigenous Peoples of the Americas;

• to present the conference documentation to the United Nations Secretary-General and to submit the conclusions and recommendations of the Conference to the appropriate organs of the United Nations;

• to study and foster the discussion of the attached Draft Declaration of Principles for the Defense of the Indigenous National and Peoples of the Western Hemisphere, elaborated by indigenous peoples' representatives;

• to take all possible measures to support and defend any participant in the conference who may face harassment and persecution on their return;

• to express to ICEM (Intergovernmental Committee for European Migration) the concerns of the Inference about the continued settlement of immigrants on the land of indigenous peoples in the Americas and urge strongly that the resources of ICEM should not be used in support of such immigrants, particularly when coming from the racist regimes of Southern Africa.

In the legal field:

• that international instruments, particularly IL0 Convention 107, be revised to remove the emphasis on integration as the main approach to indigenous problems and to reinforce the provisions in the Convention for special measures in favour of indigenous peoples;

• that the traditional law and customs of indigenous peoples should be respected, including the jurisdiction of their own forums and procedures for applying their law and customs;

• that the special relationship of indigenous peoples to their land should be understood and recognized as basic to all their beliefs, customs, traditions and culture;

• that the right should be recognized of all indigenous nations or peoples to the return and control, as a minimum, of sufficient and suitable land to enable them to live an economically viable existence in accordance with their own customs and traditions, and to make possible their full development at their own pace. In some cases larger areas may be completely valid and possible of achievement;

• that the ownership of land by indigenous peoples should be unrestricted, and should include the ownership and control of all natural resources. The lands, land rights and natural resources of indigenous peoples should not be taken, and their land rights should not be terminated or extinguished without their full and informed consent;

• that the right of indigenous peoples to own their land communally and to manage it in accordance with their own traditions and culture should be recognized internationally and nationally, and fully protected by law;

- that in appropriate cases aid should be provided to assist indigenous peoples in acquiring the land which they require;

- that legal services should be made available to indigenous peoples to assist them in establishing and maintaining their land rights;

- that all governments should grant recognition to the organizations of indigenous peoples and should enter into meaningful negotiations with them to resolve their land problems;

- that an appeal should be made to all governments of the Western Hemisphere to ratify and apply the following Conventions:

(i) Genocide Convention

(ii) Anti-Slavery Conventions

(iii) Convention on the Elimination of all Forms of Racial Discrimination

(iv) International Covenant on Economic, Social and Cultural Rights

(v) International Covenant on Civil and Political Rights

(vi) American Convention on Human Rights

In the economic field:

- that the non-governmental organizations widely publicize the results of this conference in order to mobilize support and aid for the indigenous peoples of the Western Hemisphere in their homelands;

- that conferences, seminars and colloquia be organized by NCOs, by intergovernmental bodies on all levels - regional, national, global - with the full participation of indigenous people to keep alive the issues that have come to world-wide attention at this conference, and to hear new testimony that will be presented in the future;

- to promote the establishment of a working group under the Sub-Commission on the Prevention of Discrimination and Protection of Minorities of the United Nations Commission on Human Rights;

- to request that the United Nations Special Committee on Decolonization hold hearings on all issues affecting indigenous populations;

• that the United Nations Committee on Trans-National Corporations conduct an investigation into the role of multinational corporations in the plunder and exploitation of native lands, resources, and peoples in the Americas.

In the social and cultural field:

• to promote respect for the cultural and social integrity of indigenous populations of the Americas. Such respect should be especially promoted among local and national governments and appropriate intergovernmental organizations, and be based on the conclusions enunciated in the commission report;

• to give all possible financial and moral support to efforts initiated by American Indians in defense of their culture and society, and in particular to the various education programmes launched by Indian movements. Solidarity is also requested for political prisoners and other victims of persecution on account of their participation in such indigenous movements.

Many other proposals and recommendations were made by the conference commissions. It is suggested that they be studied by NGOs for the formulation of possible action programs by them.

The Conference requests the officers of the Sub-Committee on Racism, Racial Discrimination, Apartheid and Decolonization to promote the decisions of the Conference and to receive and circulate information from NGOs about the implementation of these decisions.

•

APPENDIX G

The 1977 Geneva Conference draft declaration became, 30 years later, the basis of the historic UN Declaration on the Rights of Indigenous Peoples, passed in 2007 by the UN General Assembly with 144 yes votes and only four no votes: Canada, Australia, New Zealand, and the United States of America.

DRAFT DECLARATION OF PRINCIPLES
for the Defense of the Indigenous Nations
and Peoples of the Western Hemisphere

(1) Recognition of Indigenous nations: Indigenous people shall be accorded recognition as nations, and proper subjects of international law, provided the people concerned desire to be recognized as a nation and meet the fundament requirement of nationhood, namely: (a) having a permanent population; (b) having a defined territory; (c) having a government; (d) having the ability to enter into relations with other states.

(2) Subjects of International Law: Indigenous groups not meeting the requirements of nationhood are hereby declared to be subjects of international law and are entitled to the protection of this Declaration, provided they are identifiable groups having bonds of language, heritage, tradition, or other common identity.

(3) Guarantee of Rights: No indigenous nation or group shall be deemed to have fewer rights or lesser status for the sole reason that the nation or group has not entered into recorded treaties or agreements with any state.

(4) Accordance of Independence: Indigenous nations or groups shall be accorded such degree of independence as they may desire in accordance with international law.

(5) Treaties and Agreements: Treaties and other agreements entered into by indigenous nations or groups with other states, whether denominated as treaties or otherwise, shall be recognized and applied in the same manner and according to the same international laws and principles as the treaties and agreements entered into by their states.

(6) Abrogation of Treaties and other Rights: Treaties and agreements made with indigenous nations or groups shall not be subject to unilateral abrogation. In no event may the municipal laws of any state serve as a defense to the failure to adhere to and perform the terms of treaties and agreements made with indigenous nations or groups. Nor shall any state refuse to recognize and adhere to treaties or other agreements due to changed circumstances where the change in circumstances has been substantially caused by the state asserting that such change has occurred.

(7) Jurisdiction: No state shall assert or claim to exercise any right of jurisdiction over any indigenous nation or group unless pursuant to a valid treaty or other agreement freely made with the lawful representatives of indigenous nation or group concerned. All actions on the part of any state which derogate from the indigenous nations' or groups' right to exercise self-determination shall be the proper concern of existing international bodies.

(8) Claims to Territory: No state shall claim or retain, by right of discovery or otherwise, the territories of an indigenous nation or group, except such lands as may have been lawfully acquired by valid treaty or other cessation freely made.

(9) Settlement of Disputes: All states in the Western hemisphere shall establish through negotiations or other appropriate means a procedure for the binding settlement of disputes, claims, or other matters relating to indigenous nations or groups. Such procedures shall be mutually acceptable to the parties, fundamentally fair, and consistent with international law. All procedures presently in existence which do not have the endorsement of the indigenous nations or groups concerned, shall be ended, and new procedures shall be instituted consistent with this Declaration.

(10) National and Cultural Integrity: It shall be unlawful for any state to take or permit any action or course of conduct with respect to an indigenous nation or group which will directly or indirectly result in the destruction or disintegration of such indigenous nation or group or otherwise threaten the national or cultural integrity of such nation or group, including, but not limited to, the imposition and support of illegitimate governments and the introduction of non-

indigenous religions to indigenous peoples by non-indigenous missionaries.

(11) Environmental Protection: It shall be unlawful for any state to make or permit any action or course of conduct with respect to the territories of an indigenous nation or group which will directly or indirectly result in the destruction or deterioration of an indigenous nation or group through the effects of pollution of earth, air, water, or which in any way depletes, displaces or destroys any natural resources or other resources under the dominion of, or vital livelihood of an indigenous nation or group.

(12) Indigenous Membership: No state, through legislation, regulation, or other means, shall take actions that interfere with the sovereign power of an indigenous nation or group to determine its own membership.

(13) Conclusion: All of the rights and obligations declared herein shall be in addition to all rights and obligations existing under international law.

•

NOTES

[1] *Journal of First Voyage to America* by Christopher Columbus, New York: A. and C. Boni, 1924, 24-27.

[2] Unless otherwise noted, all graphics are from John Curl's collection of Indigenous Peoples Day archives.

[3] All photos in Chapter One are by Nancy Gorrell or from her collection, unless otherwise marked.

[4] First published in the *Berkeley Daily Planet*, October, 2012.

[5] Turtle Island Monument flyer, 1992.

[6] *Oakland Tribune,* 8/11/1992

[7] Akwesasne Notes, *Basic Call to Consciousness*, Rooseveltown, N.Y., Mohawk Nation, 1978, 1981, 2005.

[8] *Ibid.*

[9] Roxanne Dunbar-Ortiz, "The Role of the International Indigenous Movement and What the Left is Missing: What Brought Evo Morales to Power?" *CounterPunch*, February 10-12, 2006. http://www.counterpunch.org/2006/02/10/what-brought-evo-morales-to-power/

[10] The entire list of delegates can be found in the UN Document "List of Participants," Indigenous Peoples' Center for Documentation, Research and Information (DOCIP), http://www.docip.org/Online-Documentation.32.0.html

[11] "Geneva, 1977, A Report on the Hemispheric Movement of Indigenous Peoples," by José Barreiro, in *Basic Call to Consciousness*, op. cit., 55-78.

[12] *Treaty Council News*, Vol. 1, No.7, October, 1977, can also be found at Indigenous Peoples' Center for Documentation, Research and Information (DOCIP), http://www.docip.org/Online-Documentation.32.0.html The conference photos are from this document. Photographer not credited in original.

[13] Chapter Three and Appendix Six are based on:
 • John Curl, "The Dance of the Condor and the Eagle," *Terrain*, Berkeley Ecology Center, October, 1990.
 • Roxanne Dunbar-Ortiz, "Christopher Columbus and 'The Stink Hiding the Sun,' an Interview with Creek Indian Poet Joy Harjo", *Crossroads*, October, 1990, No. 3: 16-23.
 • Elizabeth Bobsy Draper, "Minga in Ecuador." *Z Magazine*, December 1990: 33-38.

• Anthony Cody and Joe Lambert, "Celebrating 500 Years of Indian Resistance: Continental Meeting of Indigenous Peoples held in Ecuador," *Unity*, August 31, 1990: 5.

• Luz Guerra, "The Encounter of the Condor and Eagle," AFSC (Texas-Arkansas-Oklahoma), *News from the American Friends Service Committee*, August, 1990, Vol.3, No. 3: 1-2.

[14] Unless otherwise stated, all photos of the Encuentro are by John Curl.

[15] All quotes are from, "The Birth of Resistance 500," by John Curl, *Huricán* (Alliance for Cultural Democracy), Vol 2, No. 1 & 2, Summer 1991, 3.

[16] Unless otherwise stated, all photos in this section are by Nancy Gorrell or from her photo collection.

[17] Flyer, 1992

[18] *National Geographic*, November, 1975, 584-625.

Made in the USA
Columbia, SC
30 September 2020

21835148R00115